Today's Cooking with

Chef Pasquale

*Quick and easy recipes from
television's popular singing chef*

Warwick Publishing

Toronto   Los Angeles

Please visit our web site:
www.pasqualeskitchen.com

"Today's Cooking with Chef Pasquale" television shows made possible by:

Kitchen Aid Canada, Whirlpool, IPC Personal Computers, Coffee Time, Kitchen Craft Cabinetry, Monarch Kitchen and Bath Centre, EKCO, Aqua Select Canada, Fortinoís, Sheraton Hotels, AcryFlek, Grohe, Braeburn Cellars, Santa Isabela, Silverthorne Vineyards Malabar, ONtv.

We acknowledge the financial support of the Government of Canada through the Book Publishing Industry Development Program for our publishing activities.

ISBN: 1-894020-64-2

Published by Warwick Publishing Inc.
162 John Street, Suite 300, Toronto, Ontario, Canada M5V 2E5

Cover design and layout: Heidi Gemmill
Editor: Lisa Carpino

Printed and bound in Canada.

Table of Contents

Dedication

I dedicate this book to my beloved mother, Teresina, and grandmother, Carolina, and to all my dear and beautiful friends all over the world who have followed me for many years.

And to my daughter, Lisa, of whom I am especially proud because as editor of this book she put my thoughts into words.

Thanks for the tremendous support of my beloved wife Evelyna and my daughter Beatrice. My heart and love go out to my brothers Antonio, Giovanni, Carmine, Mario, and sister Anna and their families.

Special thanks to Jim Williamson of Warwick, who has been my publisher and best friend for 20 years. Thanks also to Fred Cimato of Max Media Productions, Beth McBlain, and Larry Schnurr of ONTV, the producers of my television show.

Foreword

Cooking is an art, and as with most arts, there is a high level of creativity involved. In this collection, exact quantities are given for the ingredients needed in each recipe. It will not surprise you to know, however, that most chefs measure correct amounts with their eyes more often than with their hands. Some days it's a little less, some days a little more. Just as a song cannot be sung exactly the same way twice, so a recipe cannot be repeated. So, unless you are baking a cake, don't worry too much about measuring to the very last milligram. In cooking, it is more important how the chosen ingredients blend together and complement each other. The right combination of ingredients will make a beautiful recipe, just as the right combination of notes makes a beautiful melody.

By the same token, if a certain recipe calls for an ingredient that you really do not like or cannot find, then substitute it with a similar one that works just as well. For example, you can use bacon instead of pancetta, or green onion instead of red onion, or spinach instead of rapini. Feel free to adjust seasonings to your own taste.

Recipes must be as individual as you are. These recipes are from my kitchen and so, reflect me. But I offer them into your kitchen now, where they will become your own.

Buon'appetito!

Italian Cooking

The Classic Italian Meal

In Italy, food is central to cultural and family life, so it makes sense that the focal point of social gatherings is often the dinner table. A meal doesn't always have to be an elaborate affair, but for special occasions and feasts, these are the courses of a traditional Italian meal. They are more fully explained under each individual chapter heading.

Antipasti

These are the appetizers served before the main meal. They are meant to entice the palate and prepare it for the following courses.

Primo Piatto

This is the first course, which normally includes soup, pasta, risotto, gnocchi, or polenta served in small portions.

Piatto di Mezzo

This is the main course or entrée. The menu will include fish, poultry, game, meat or an egg dish.

Contorni

These are the vegetables or side dishes. They may be served along with the main course, but always on a separate plate.

Insalata Verde

Salad comes at the end of a meal and is meant to cleanse the palate.

Formaggio e Frutta Fresca

After the meal and before the dessert, a selection of fine cheese and fresh fruit is served. This sometimes takes the place of dessert.

Dolci

This is usually a sweet and simple dessert.

Caffe

Coffee and a fine liqueur are the perfect way to end a delicious meal.

Herbs and Spices
Erbe Aromatica e Spezie

Herbs and spices add flavour and scent to both savoury and sweet dishes and are indispensable in Italian cooking. Whenever possible, you should try to use fresh seasonings, but dried and powdered can be substituted. A good rule of thumb is to use about 1/2 teaspoon (2 ml) of powdered or 1 teaspoon (5 ml) of dried to every tablespoon (15 ml) of fresh minced seasoning.

Here is a selection of seasonings commonly found in Italian cooking and in this cookbook.

Anise / *Anice*

Native to the Mediterranean, the seeds (aniseed) are often used in baking, particularly in *biscotti* (biscuits) and *panettone* (Easter egg bread).

Basil / *Basilico*

This herb is most associated with Italian cooking. It is extremely aromatic and has a warm, minty flavour. It is used in pesto, salads and tomato sauce. Six leaves of fresh basil is equal to 1 tsp. (5 ml) of dried.

Bay / *Alloro*

This Mediterranean evergreen has a pungent flavour and aroma that has been described as woodsy, peppery and even lemony. It is good with meat, soups, stews and sauces.

Black peppercorn / *Pepe in Grana*

This sharp spice is used in savoury dishes like Spaghetti Carbonara. It is best freshly ground.

Cinnamon / *Cannella*

Available ground or in stick form. A sweet, aromatic spice used mainly in desserts or sprinkled on cappuccino.

Chili pepper / *Peperoncino*

Fresh chili pepper is strong and hot, as are red pepper flakes that are made from dried and crushed chili peppers. Use sparingly. Chili powder is a mix of dried chilies, garlic, oregano, coriander, cumin, and cloves, and can be mild or hot. If your hands come in contact with chili pepper in any form, wash them immediately before you accidentally rub your eyes or nose.

Clove / *Garofano*

Warm and spicy. Available ground or whole. Mostly used to season meat and poultry and desserts.

Fennel / *Finocchio*

Both the leaves and the seeds have an anise flavour. Fennel is good with fish, pork, and vegetables.

Ginger / *Zenzero*

Sharp and lemony. Not commonly found in Italian cooking, but a nice addition to spicy dishes.

Marjoram / *Maggiorana*

Spicy and fresh. Used in tomato sauces, soups, and fish dishes.

Mustard / *Senape*

Hot and peppery. Used as a dried powder or as a prepared paste in Italian cooking. Good in sauces, salads, and meats, especially roast beef and ham.

Mint / *Menta*

Crisp and refreshing. Good with lamb, vegetables, salads and fruit.

Nutmeg / *Noce Moscata*

Warm and musky. Used in a variety of cream sauces and sweets. It is the secret of a good tomato sauce.

Oregano / *Origano*

Known as wild marjoram. Spicy and aromatic, stronger than marjoram and even more intense when dried. Used sparingly in antipasto, soups, sauces, and, of course, pizza.

Paprika / *Paprica*

A mixture of ground red sweet peppers, milder than chili pepper. Good with fish and vegetables.

Parsley / *Prezzemolo*

Flat-leaf Italian parsley is fresh and pungent. Good in any savoury dish, and nice as a garnish. Parsley is best added at the end of cooking time, just before you are ready to serve the dish.

Rosemary / *Rosamarino*

Strong and aromatic. Used sparingly in poultry, game, pork and lamb dishes.

Saffron / *Zafferano*

A warm-bitter flavour and golden colour. Used sparingly.

Sage / *Salvia*

Woodsy and aromatic. This herb is native to the Mediterranean. Used in stuffing and in veal and pork dishes.

Tarragon / *Dragoncello*

A slight anise flavour. Good with chicken, fish, salads and sauces. Use fresh whenever possible.

Thyme / *Timo*

This spicy and aromatic herb is native to the Mediterranean. Goes well with chicken, beef, pork, lamb, stews and marinades.

Italian Cheese
Formaggi

Italians love cheese and have incorporated it into many aspects of a meal. It can be enjoyed as an antipasto accompanied by a fine wine, as a topping for countless dishes, as an ingredient in sauces, or even as a treat served with fruit after supper. Here is a selection of the finest Italian cheeses.

Asiago

A sharp and rich cow's milk cheese made from whole or part skim milk. Young asiago is delicious with fresh fruit after a meal. Aged asiago, which is sharper, can be grated and added to savoury dishes.

Bel Paese

A mild, soft cow's milk cheese from Lombardy. Makes a lovely dessert cheese.

Caciocavallo

A sharp, firm cow's milk cheese produced in the south of Italy. Its name ("horse cheese") comes from its being hung in pairs to dry on either side of a pole, as if on horseback.

Crotonese

A slightly peppery cheese made from sheep and goat's milk in Calabria. Good for grating and also goes well with fruit at the end of a meal.

Fontina

A mild, semi-soft cheese made from whole cow's milk in Piedmont. This smooth, delicately flavoured cheese is often melted, but is also a delicious snack.

Friulano

A mild, firm table cheese made from part skim milk. Great for sandwiches and snacks.

Gorgonzola

A rich blue cheese made from cow's milk. This popular, strong-smelling cheese is usually crumbled into salads or pizza, or melted into sauces.

Mascarpone

A fresh cow's milk cream cheese from the Lombardy region. The rich, creamy cheese is similar in consistency to a soft cream cheese or a smooth ricotta. It is mostly used in desserts.

Mozzarella

A mild, fresh cheese made from cow's or buffalo's milk. It is a good melting cheese because of its soft and stringy texture when heated. It is most often used in pizza and lasagna or marinated for antipasto. You can also find fresh mozzarella packed in water or whey and shaped into little balls called bocconcini.

Parmigiano

Also called **Parmesan**. A hard cow's milk cheese most often grated. The tastiest variety of this salty cheese is the **Parmigiano-Reggiano**, which is aged for at least one year. Delicious on pasta, risotto, and in sauces.

Pecorino

A sharp, hard grating cheese made from fresh ewe's milk. Used as a table cheese, much like Parmesan. The best known is **Pecorino Romano**, which is aged for about 8 months.

Provolone

A firm, lightly smoked cow's milk cheese. It is available *dolce* (sweet) or *piccante* (spicy), which is stronger and sharper. A delicious cheese for snacking, grating, or slicing.

Ricotta

A fresh, moist cow's milk cheese made from the whey, traditionally made from ewe's milk. Similar to cottage cheese but creamier. Considered somewhat of a delicacy in Italy and often sprinkled with sugar and eaten as a dessert. Available in whole milk and part skim varieties.

Italian Cured Meat

Cured meats are widely used in all aspects of Italian cooking, from sauces and stuffing to antipasto and sandwich fillings. Most varieties are made from pork and are salt-cured and air-dried.

Capocollo

Salt-cured pork shoulder or neck seasoned with ground pepper, paprika, salt and sugar. Similar to prosciutto, but less fatty. Usually sliced thinly and served as a cold cut or appetizer.

Mortadella

Sausage made of finely ground pork meat with fat and spices added, such as peppercorn. Usually sliced thinly as a cold meat or appetizer.

Pancetta

Salted and cured Italian bacon made from the pork flank. Used mainly as flavouring for a variety of dishes. If you cannot find it, bacon may be substituted.

Prosciutto

Dry-cured leg of pork which is treated to a long curing and aging process. Usually sliced paper thin for antipasto or added to meat fillings and pasta dishes.

Salami

Large sausage made mainly from ground pork, although sometimes other meats are added. Flavours differ depending on the coarseness and seasonings. **Soppressata** (compressed pork) is one type of salami flavoured with various seasonings and aged until hard. Usually served cold for antipasto, salads or sandwiches.

Salsiccie / Sausages

Italians make some of the finest homemade pork sausages and every region has its own type. For example, **ventricina** is a pork sausage from Abruzzo that is seasoned with fennel and chili pepper. Sausages can be fresh or air-dried and are cased in animal intestines.

Other Ingredients

There are many ingredients that are commonly used in Italian cooking. Here are some that will appear in many of my recipes and that you might want to keep on hand in your pantry.

Anchovies / *Acciughe*

This tasty fish is available filleted and canned and ready to eat. They are sometimes salted or else marinated in olive oil and lemon juice and eaten raw. Anchovy paste is called *pasta d'acciuga* and can also be used in sauces, on pizza, or to season a variety of dishes.

Artichoke Hearts / *Cuori di Carciofi*

Artichoke hearts consist of the choke and tender inner leaves. These delicious morsels are available marinated in oil, vinegar, salt and spices. They are normally served as part of an antipasto dish, but can be added to salads and other dishes.

Balsamic Vinegar / *Aceto Balsamico*

This dark vinegar has a smooth, sweet-sour flavour. Made from the sweet, boiled-down must of white Trebbiano grapes. It is aged in a series of at least five barrels, each made of different wood. The longest aged balsamics are the most expensive and the better tasting, but cheaper ones are suitable for everyday cooking.

Beans / *Fagioli*

One of the oldest staples in the human diet. Italians eat a variety of both Old World and New World beans. The former are eaten shelled and include **fava beans** (*fave* — what North Americans call broad beans), **lentils** (*lenticchie*) and **chickpeas** (*ceci*). New World beans, which came to Europe in the 16th century, include **green beans** (*fagiolini*), which are eaten unshelled, and other shelled varieties like **kidney beans** (*cannellini*).

Bell peppers / *Peperoni*

These sweet peppers can be found in a variety of colours — yellow, orange, red and green, which is the unripe version. Whatever the colour, they are all tasty and add a lot of character to sauces and savoury dishes.

Butter / *Burro*

Butter is used more often in northern Italy where there is better grazing land and more cows. I use it in many of my recipes because it adds a rich, subtle taste. It can be used in combination with olive oil or vegetable oil, or on its own.

Capers / *Capperi*

Capers are the young flower buds of the *Capparis spinosa* shrub. They come pickled in brine and have a tangy, pungent flavour. Great with marinated antipasti and with fish, especially smoked salmon.

Cornmeal / *Farina Gialla*

Made from dried corn kernels. It comes in yellow and white and the coarseness of grain varies. Polenta is cooked cornmeal.

Cornstarch or Potato Starch / *Fecola di Patate*

A starch made from corn or potatoes and used as a thickening agent for sauces, stews, custards and puddings in place of flour and fat.

Cream / *Panna*

Panna refers to heavy cream, which produces the best results when added to sauces. Light cream or even table cream might curdle when combined with other ingredients and heated. If you are unable to include cream in your diet, one alternative is to use scalded milk in recipes that call for cream.

Eggplant / *Melanzana*

There are countless varieties of eggplant available. To rid eggplants of their bitterness before adding to a recipe, you should salt them for about 1 hour. This will allow the bitter juices to drain from the eggplant. Just remember to rinse them off afterwards or they will be too salty. Eggplants may also be dried or preserved in oil.

Espresso

This finely ground dark roast coffee is great to keep on hand not only for making espresso, but also for desserts and sauces. The coffee is made when steam is forced at high pressure through the ground beans, a method which produces a very strong brew. It is served black in a *demitasse* and if it is made well, it should have a slight foam on the surface known as the *schiuma*. Don't confuse this with the foam on cappuccino, which is produced with milk. If you want a *caffe corretto,* you can serve your espresso with a shot of grappa or brandy.

Fig / *Fico*

Sweet and delicious, this popular Mediterranean fruit is usually eaten raw or accompanied by prosciutto for antipasto.

Fennel Bulb / *Finocchio*

This crisp bulb has a sharp anise flavour. It is related to celery and can be eaten as a vegetable, either raw or cooked.

Garlic / *Aglio*

This is one of the essential seasonings in Italian cooking. Garlic comes in a head or bulb that is made up of individual cloves. Choose heads that are firm and unblemished and that are not sprouting any green shoots.

Greens / *Verdura*

The greens native to Italy add a distinctive taste to soups, salads, and antipasto and are delicious steamed or braised. The varieties include **broccoli rabe** (*rapini*), **chicory** (*cicoria*), **curly endive** (*indivia*), **dandelion greens** (*dente di leone*), **escarole** (*scarola*), **radicchio**, which is a bitter, red leaf chicory, and **Swiss chard** (*bietola*), which is thought to be native to Italy.

Mushrooms / *Funghi*

Wild and cultivated mushrooms can be found in a vast array of Italian recipes. A few of these varieties are available year-round in North American grocery stores. The **cremini**, or Italian brown mushroom, is related to the white button mushroom and has a smooth, round cap. **Ceppetelli** (oyster mushrooms) are shell-shaped and greyish in colour with a smooth texture. **Porcini** is a prized mushroom, plump and meaty. It is also available dried and can be re-hydrated by being soaked in warm water for 30 minutes, rinsed and squeezed. **Portobello** mushrooms are grown-up cremini mushrooms and are large and meaty.

Nuts / *Noci*

Regional recipes often incorporate various nuts, especially ones that are abundant in or native to a particular area. Some popular Italian nuts are **almonds** (*mandorle*), **chestnuts** (*castagne*), which are used in many desserts, **pine nuts** (*pinoli*), which are used in pesto, **hazelnuts** (*nocciole*), which are used in both sweet and savoury dishes, and **pistachios.**

Olive / *Oliva*

One of the most important Mediterranean crops and exports. Ripe olives are black and tender, while green olives are the unripened ones that have been pickled in brine. You can also find them stuffed with pimentos or anchovies. Both are excellent in antipasto dishes, as snacks, and the black olives made a nice addition to many recipes.

Olive Oil / *Olio di Oliva*

Olive oil is used mainly in the southern regions of Italy where the climate is ideal for growing olives. If you are going to use olive oil uncooked, or in a dish where the flavour will stand out, extra virgin olive oil is the best choice. This oil is taken from the first pressing of the olives and has less than 1% acidity. It should be a golden green colour with a strong aroma and a distinct olive flavour. Virgin or pure olive oils or a good vegetable oil can be substituted in most recipes.

Onion / *Cipolla*

Many types of onion can be used in Italian cooking and you may use whichever you prefer. **Pearl onions** or **small white onions** (*cipolline*) are often pickled for antipasto, but can also be tossed into stews. **Cooking onions**, like the yellow-skinned variety, are excellent because they don't become too sweet or soft when cooked. **Sweet onions** like Bermuda, Spanish, Red, and Italian are mild enough to be eaten raw, but are not as good for cooking. **Green onions** or **scallions** (*scalogni*) taste like chives and make a nice addition to salads, sauces, and soups. Choose onions that are firm and unblemished, with dry, shiny skin and no sprouts.

Persimmon / *Kaki or Cachi*

This is one of Italy's most popular fruits. Very sweet and reddish-orange when ripe. Often sliced and served with prosciutto for antipasto.

Pesto

Literally translated as "pounded" or "crushed," mashed with mortar and pestle. This aromatic green paste is made from fresh basil leaves, olive oil, pine nuts or walnuts, garlic and Pecorino (Romano) or Parmesan cheese, a recipe associated with Genoa.

Summer Squash / *Zucchini*

In Italian, the word zucchini is a diminutive of *zucca* (gourd or squash). Zucchini is very versatile and can be grilled, marinated, or stuffed. Fried zucchini flowers are particularly delicious.

Tomato / *Pomodoro*

First described as "golden apples" (*pomi d'oro*) in the 16th century, tomatoes are now used in many ways in an Italian kitchen. You can buy them fresh, canned whole, preserved as a sauce, as a paste, or sun-dried. If you are buying them fresh, make sure they are red and smooth-skinned with no cracks or bruises. The best variety for making sauce or for home preserving is the **Roma or plum tomato** because it produces a thick, meaty sauce. Canned plum tomatoes are also fine for making sauce. **Tomato paste** (*concentrato di pomodoro*) can be added to thicken a sauce if the tomatoes are too liquid. **Sun-dried tomatoes** (*pomodori seccati*) have become very popular in recent years. They can be re-hydrated by being soaked in warm water for 30 minutes and squeezed to drain the excess liquid.

Wine / *Vino*

When using red or white wine in cooking, choose one that you would also enjoy drinking by itself because the taste will not change once it is cooked with the food. **Marsala** is a fortified dessert wine which ranges from very sweet to very dry. It is excellent with meat and in sauces and desserts.

Wine Vinegar / *Aceto di Vino*

Widely used in Italian cooking. Made from good white, red or rosé wines which are fermented until sour and acidic. A tasty vinegar for salads and antipasto.

Fresh Preserves

This section contains recipes for preserving fresh herbs and vegetables. Oil is used as the preserving agent in all of these recipes. They are designed for storage in the freezer so that you may use them year-round, no matter what the season.

Not only are these preserves delicious, but they also save you time in the long run. A few minutes of using the food processor creates a fresh seasoning that will last for 4 months in the freezer. Whenever you need some minced garlic, or chopped herbs, or freshly squeezed lemon juice, the only instrument you'll need is a spoon to drop in a bit of your preserve.

Just remember that if you are using olive oil for any of the recipes, make sure it is petrified olive oil. Otherwise, vegetable or corn oil is your best choice, as it stays soft when frozen. Many of the recipes in this book incorporate these preserves. If you do not wish to use them in your own cooking, simply substitute them with the fresh ingredients listed in their recipes, minus the oil. For example, if a recipe calls for 1 tablespoon of my fresh basil preserve, simply substitute that with a tablespoon of freshly chopped basil.

Conserva Aromatica
Aromatic Preserve

This preserved sauce goes well with pasta and risotto, or can be used as a dressing for salads, boiled vegetables and meat.

Fresh basil leaves	1 cup	250 ml
Flat leaf parsley	3/4 cup	180 ml
Fresh rosemary leaves	1/4 cup	60 ml
Fresh oregano leaves	1/4 cup	60 ml
Fresh sage leaves	1/4 cup	60 ml
Vegetable oil	2 cups	500 ml
Red chili peppers	2	2
Garlic cloves, peeled	4	4
Dried marjoram	2 tbsp.	30 ml
Dried thyme	2 tbsp.	30 ml
Ginger powder	2 tbsp.	30 ml
Salt	1 tbsp.	15 ml

Place all ingredients in food processor; this may have to be done in batches. Process until smooth. To preserve, pour into a freezer-proof jar or plastic container and freeze immediately. It will keep for 6 months in your freezer.

Makes about 4 cups/1 litre.

Conserva di Basilico Fresco
Fresh Basil Preserve

This basil condiment can be added to sauces, soups, and dressings for a little hint of freshness.

Basil leaves and the tender part of the stems, chopped	1 1/2 cup	375 ml
Vegetable or olive oil	1 cup	250 ml
Garlic cloves, peeled (optional)	6	6
Salt	1 tsp.	5 ml

Place the basil, oil, garlic, and salt in a food processor and blend for 2 minutes, until smooth. Use right away or pour into a freezer-proof container and store in the freezer for 6 months.

Makes 2 cups/500 ml.

Conserva di Peperoncino
Chili Pepper Preserve

This chili pepper condiment can be added to barbecue or pasta sauce.

Red chili pepper, cored	1 lb.	450 g
Flat leaf parsley, chopped	1/2 cup	120 ml
Green onions, sliced	4	4
Vegetable or olive oil	1 1/2 cup	375 ml
Salt	1 tsp.	5 ml

Combine all ingredients in a food processor or blender and blend for 2 minutes, or until smooth. Use right away or pour into freezer-proof jars and store in the freezer for 6 months.

Makes 3 cups/750 ml.

Conserva di Erba Cipollina
Fresh Chive Preserve

This preserve makes a great addition to sauces, salad dressings and soups, and tastes great on fish and poultry.

Fresh chives, coarsely chopped	1 cup	250 ml
Fresh parsley, coarsely chopped	1 cup	250 ml
Vegetable oil	1 1/2 cup	375 ml
White wine (optional)	1/2 cup	120 ml
Pickling salt	2 tbsp.	30 ml

Combine all ingredients in a food processor or blender. Blend for 2 minutes or until smooth. Use right away or pour into a freezer-proof container and store in the freezer for up to 4 months.

Makes 3 to 4 cups/750 ml to 1 litre.

Conserva d'Aglio Fresco
Fresh Garlic Preserve

This is a great condiment to have on hand in the freezer. You can use it in any recipe calling for garlic, without any chopping or cleaning up to do.

Garlic heads, peeled	6	6
Vegetable oil	2 cups	500 ml
White wine	1 cup	250 ml
Lemon juice	1 cup	250 ml
Salt	1 tbsp.	15 ml

Combine all ingredients in a food processor and blend for 2 minutes, until smooth. Use right away or pour into freezer-proof containers and store in the freezer for 6 months.

Makes about 4 cups/1 litre.

Conserva di Cipollina Verde, Cipolla Rossa e Bianca
Fresh Green, Red and White Onion Preserve

This is a great condiment to keep on hand in the freezer. You can use it in any recipe calling for onions, without having to worry about your eyes watering.

Green onions, chopped	8 to 10	8 to 10
Red onion, diced	1	1
White onion, diced	1	1
Sunflower oil	2 cups	500 ml
Corn oil	1 cup	250 ml
White wine	1 cup	250 ml
Fresh lemon juice	1/2 cup	120 ml
Salt	1 tbsp.	15 ml

Combine all ingredients in a food processor and blend for 2 minutes, until smooth. Use right away or pour into freezer-proof containers and store in the freezer for 6 months.

Makes about 6 cups/1 1/2 litres.

Conserva di Limone
Fresh Lemon Preserve

If you don't have fresh lemons on hand, this is a handy alternative to keep in your freezer. It also makes a good marinade for fish.

Lemons, peeled, seeded and chopped	8	8
Italian parsley, coarsely chopped	1/2 cup	120 ml
Corn oil	2 cups	500 ml
White wine	1 cup	250 ml
Salt and pepper, to taste		

Place all ingredients in a food processor and blend until smooth. Use right away, or pour into freezer-proof containers and store in the freezer for 6 months.

Makes about 4 cups/1 litre.

Pesto
Basil Garlic Herb Paste

This version of pesto is designed for preserving in a large quantity. If you are making fresh pesto to be used immediately, use olive oil instead of corn oil.

Fresh basil, coarsely chopped	4 oz.	115 g
Pine nuts or walnuts	8 oz.	225 g
Garlic cloves, peeled	8	8
Corn oil	1 1/2 cups	375 ml
Salt and pepper, to taste		
Parmesan cheese	1 cup	250 ml

In a food processor, combine basil, pine nuts, garlic, oil, salt and pepper. Blend for 1 minute, or until creamy and smooth. At this point, you may pour mixture into freezer-proof jars and freeze for later use. To serve, mix in the Parmesan cheese. A good rule of thumb for pasta is to use 3 tbsp. (45 ml) of pesto per person, mixed with 3 tbsp. (45 ml) of Parmesan cheese, and 1 tbsp.(15 ml) of butter, if desired.

Makes about 3 cups/750 ml.

Conserva di Pomodori Secchi
Sun-Dried Tomato Preserve

This preserve is a great addition to tomato sauce, pizza sauce, meat sauce, soups and risotto.

Sun-dried tomatoes	1/3 cup	90 ml
Vegetable oil	2 cups	500 ml
Onion, peeled and quartered	1	1
Garlic cloves (optional)	3	3
Nutmeg, grated	1 tsp.	5 ml
Salt	1 tsp.	5 ml

Soak the sun-dried tomatoes in hot water for 10 minutes to reconstitute them. Squeeze off any excess liquid. Combine all ingredients in a food processor or blender. Blend until smooth, about 1 to 2 minutes. Use right away or store in a freezer-proof container in the freezer for 3 months.

Tip: Use 1/4 cup (60 ml) of preserve for every 2 quarts (2 litres) of sauce.

Makes about 3 cups/750 ml.

Conserva di Porcini
Porcini Mushroom Preserve

This preserve makes a nice addition to pasta sauce, risotto, meat and soups.

Dried Porcini mushrooms	1/4 cup	60 ml
Corn oil	1 1/2 cups	375 ml
Green onions, chopped	4	4
Garlic cloves (optional)	2	2
Salt	1 tsp.	5 ml

Soak dried mushrooms in hot water for 8 minutes to reconstitute them. Squeeze out any excess liquid.Combine all ingredients in a food processor or blender. Blend until smooth, about 1 to 2 minutes. Use right away or pour into a freezer-proof container and store in the freezer for 2 to 3 months.

Tip: Use 1/4 cup (60 ml) of preserve for every quart (litre) of sauce.

Makes about 2 1/2 cups/ 620 ml.

Condimento per Pesci e Pollame
Seasoning for Fish and Poultry

This condiment can be used to marinate poultry, fish, game, pork, veal or lamb. The ratio for a marinade would be 1 tbsp. (15 ml) of seasoning for every 1 1/2 lbs. (680 g) of meat.

Fresh sage leaves	3/4 cup	180 ml
Fresh oregano leaves	1/2 cup	120 ml
Fresh rosemary leaves	1/2 cup	120 ml
Vegetable oil	2 cups	500 ml
Lemon juice	1/2 cup	120 ml
De-alcoholized wine	1/2 cup	120 ml
Garlic cloves, peeled	2	2
The peel of 1 lemon		
Salt	1 tsp.	5 ml

Combine all ingredients in a food processor and blend for 3 to 4 minutes, until rich and smooth. Use right away or pour into freezer-proof containers and store in the freezer for 6 months.

Makes 6 cups/1 1/2 litres.

Sauces and Condiments

The proper sauces and condiments are essential to successful recipes. They must be complementary to the other ingredients so that they blend in well, yet not so that they lose their own character. Sometimes they alone can make the dish. Here are some classic sauces and condiments common to most kitchens. You will find recipes for salad dressings in the salad section.

Salsa Bruna
Gravy

This large-batch recipe can be made with or without the fat.

Butter or vegetable oil	3/4 cup	180 ml
Flour or cornstarch	1/3 cup	90 ml
Tomato paste	2 tbsp.	30 ml
Red wine	3/4 cup	180 ml
Beef stock	2 quarts	2 litres
Cold water	3/4 cup	180 ml
Salt and pepper to taste		

Method 1 (with fat):

In a saucepan, melt butter over medium heat; add flour, stirring constantly until roux turns dark brown in colour. Mix in tomato paste and remove from heat. When sauce has cooled a bit, add wine, stock, salt and pepper. Bring back to boil and let simmer for about 10 minutes. Strain and serve.

Method 2 (without fat):

Combine stock, tomato paste, wine, salt and pepper in saucepan and bring to a boil. Dilute flour or cornstarch in water (broth or wine can be substituted) and add to the stock. Let boil for 5 minutes, stirring constantly. Strain and serve.

Tip: This method can also be used for other meat gravies, including veal, lamb, pork, chicken turkey, and game.

Makes about 8 cups/2 litres.

Besciamella
Béchamel Sauce

Homo or 2% milk	1 quart	1 litre
Chicken broth (see recipe, p. 39)	1/2 cup	120 ml
Butter	3/4 cup	180 ml
Olive oil	1/4 cup	60 ml
All-purpose flour	1/3 cup	90 ml
Scallions, finely chopped	1/2 cup	120 ml
Nutmeg, grated	1/2 tsp.	2 ml
Salt and pepper, to taste		

In a medium saucepan, bring milk and chicken broth to a boil. In another saucepan, combine butter, oil, flour, onions, and seasoning. Mix thoroughly to form a roux. Add the boiling milk mixture, stirring constantly until sauce is thick and creamy. Adjust liquid amount, if necessary.

Makes about 4 cups/1 litre.

Salsa Olandese
Hollandaise Sauce

This is the perfect accompaniment to fish and vegetable dishes.

Egg yolks	6	6
Dry mustard	4 tbsp.	60 ml
Lemon juice	1/2 cup	120 ml
Cayenne pepper	1 tsp.	5 ml
Clarified butter or olive oil	1 1/2 lbs.	675 g
Sherry	1/2 cup	120 ml
Salt and pepper, to taste		

In a stainless steel saucepan, combine egg yolks, mustard, lemon juice, cayenne. Whisk over medium low heat until eggs thicken. Remove from heat and continue to whisk as you add in the clarified butter.

Tip: Place the pan on a wet towel to prevent it from shifting as you whisk.

Mix in sherry and adjust seasoning to taste with salt and pepper. Strain through cheesecloth, if necessary, to remove any bits of cooked egg.

Makes about 2 cups/500 ml.

Maionese
Mayonnaise

For easier whisking, place a wet towel under your bowl. This will prevent any shifting.

Egg yolks	5	5
Prepared mustard	4 tbsp.	60 ml
Lemon juice	1/2 cup	120 ml
Cayenne pepper, or hot pepper sauce	1/2 tsp.	2 ml
Olive oil	3 cups	750 ml
White vinegar	1/3 cup	90 ml
Water	1/2 cup	120 ml
Salt and pepper to taste		

In a stainless steel bowl, combine egg yolks, mustard, lemon juice, and cayenne. Whisk in one direction until eggs thicken. Slowly add half the oil in a thin stream and continue whisking until mixture is thick and creamy. In a small pot, bring vinegar and water to a boil. Slowly add to the egg mixture, along with the remaining oil. The heat will slightly cook the eggs and allow you to store the mayonnaise for a longer period of time. Adjust the flavour with salt and pepper to taste. Refrigerate immediately.

Makes about 4 cups/1 litre.

Salsa per Pesce al Freddo
Cocktail Sauce

This dipping sauce is perfect for any cold fish salad or cocktail.

Ketchup	2 cups	500 ml
Horseradish	1 cup	250 ml
Olive oil	1 cup	250 ml
Lemon juice	1/2 cup	120 ml
White vinegar	1/2 cup	120 ml
Sugar	1/4 cup	60 ml
Tomato paste	2 tbsp.	30 ml
Prepared mustard	2 tbsp.	30 ml
Hot pepper sauce	1 tbsp.	15 ml
Salt and pepper		
Worcestershire sauce (optional)		

Combine all ingredients in a large bowl and whisk for 3 to 5 minutes. Keep tightly sealed in refrigerator.

Makes about 6 cups/1 1/2 litres.

Salsa alla Crema
Basic Cream Sauce

Butter	1/4 cup	60 ml
Oil	1/4 cup	60 ml
All purpose flour	1/3 cup	90 ml
Milk	1 quart	1 litre
Chicken stock	1/2 cup	120 ml
White wine (optional)	1/2 cup	120 ml
Nutmeg, grated	1 tsp.	5 ml
Salt and pepper		

In a medium pot, heat butter and oil over medium heat. Stir in flour to make a roux and cook for 4 to 6 minutes, stirring constantly. Scald the milk and add along with remaining ingredients to roux. Bring to a boil and simmer until thickened.

Makes about 4 cups/1 litre.

Salsa al Pomodoro
Basic Tomato Sauce

This basic sauce can be used for pasta, risotto, stews and casseroles.

Vegetable oil	1/4 cup	60 ml
Medium onion, diced	1	1
Garlic cloves, minced	2	2
Tomatoes, peeled and diced	2 quarts	2 litres
Olive oil	1/4 cup	60 ml
Fresh basil leaves, coarsely chopped	6	6
Fresh bay leaves, crushed	2	2
Pinch of nutmeg		
Salt and pepper		

In a medium saucepan, heat oil and sauté onion and garlic until translucent. Add remaining ingredients, except olive oil, and bring to boil. Adjust temperature to low heat and simmer for 30 minutes, stirring occasionally.

Tip: As the tomatoes cook, foam will appear on the surface of the liquid. When this foam disappears, it is a sign that your tomatoes are properly cooked. Add the olive oil and serve.

Makes about 6 cups/1 1/2 litres.

Salsa Arrabbiata
Hot Tomato Sauce

This spicy sauce is translated as "angry style" and is used for the traditional Pasta all' Arrabbiata. It also tastes great on pizza, rice, and meat dishes.

Olive oil	1/3 cup	90 ml
Red onion, chopped	1 cup	250 ml
Garlic cloves, minced	3	3
Chili peppers, chopped	1 cup	250 ml
Mushrooms, sliced	6	6
Tomatoes, peeled	1 quart	1 litre
Red wine	1/2 cup	120 ml
Red wine vinegar	1/4 cup	60 ml
Lemon juice	1/4 cup	60 ml
Chili pepper preserve (see recipe, p. 18)	1/4 cup	60 ml
Fresh basil preserve (see recipe, p. 18)	1 tbsp.	15 ml
Salt and pepper, to taste		

In a saucepan, heat oil and sauté onion, garlic, peppers, and mushrooms for 4 minutes. Lower heat to medium and add remaining ingredients. Simmer for 20 minutes, stirring occasionally, or until the froth disappears. You may serve this immediately or cool and store in tightly covered jars in the refrigerator for up to two weeks.

Makes about 4 cups/1 litre.

Pastella per Pesci e Vegetali
Batter for Fish and Vegetables

This tempura batter can be used for deep-frying vegetables and fish.

All purpose flour	2 cups	500 ml
Flat beer or 2% milk	1 cup	250 ml
Eggs	2	2
Vegetable oil	1/4 cup	60 ml
Sugar	1 tbsp.	15 ml
Baking powder	1 tbsp.	15 ml
Salt	1 tsp.	5 ml

In a large bowl, whisk together all ingredients until batter reaches a consistency similar to pancake batter. If too thick, add more milk; if too thin, add more flour. Allow the batter to rest for 3 to 4 hours before you begin frying.

Tip: for excellent results when deep-frying, always make sure the temperature of your oil is 325°F (160°C).

Makes about 3 1/2 cups/875 ml.

Salsa per Pizza
Pizza Sauce

Vegetable oil	1/3 cup	90 ml
Onion, chopped	1	1
Garlic cloves, minced	2	2
Tomatoes, strained	1 quart	1 litre
Dried basil	2 tbsp.	30 ml
Dried oregano	2 tbsp.	30 ml
Chopped parsley	2 tbsp.	30 ml
Sugar	2 tbsp.	30 ml
Nutmeg, grated	1 tsp.	5 ml
Salt and pepper, to taste		

In a saucepan, heat oil and sauté onion, garlic and herbs for 2 minutes.
Add remaining ingredients and simmer over moderate heat for 15 to 20 minutes, stirring occasionally. This sauce may be refrigerated for up to two weeks.

Makes about 3 cups/750 ml.

Antipasto

Antipasto is an Italian term for appetizer, or *hors d'oeuvre*, translated literally as "before the meal." The *antipasti*, or appetizers, are served as a small, savoury first course, bits to nibble on before the main meal.

An *antipasto* dish, like the overture to an opera, is meant to entice the palate and encourage our appetites for that which is still to come.

Typically, you would serve a variety of foods that are fresh and in season, arranged in an attractive manner. After all, the *antipasto* should entice your eyes as well as your taste buds. A selection of marinated vegetables and fish, sliced cheese, cold cuts and perhaps fruit is called *antipasto misto* (mixed appetizer). A selection of sliced cured meats is *antipasto affettato* (sliced appetizer).

A good host or hostess will offer some aperitifs to accompany the selection of appetizers. An aperitif, or *aperitivo*, is typically an alcoholic drink taken before a meal to stimulate the appetite. Some popular Italian aperitifs are:

Asti Spumante

A sweet, sparkling wine made from Muscat grapes. This is Italy's version of champagne.

Campari

A red, bittersweet spirit made from citrus and herbs. Often mixed with soda water or orange juice.

Vermouth

A fortified wine flavoured with herbs, spices, and fruit peel. Available red or white, sweet or dry.

Bruschetta
Garlic Bread

Crusty Italian bread works best for this appetizer.

Italian bread slices, about 1 inch (2.5 cm) thick	8	8
Garlic cloves, halved	4	4
Olive oil	3/4 cup	180 ml
Crushed peppercorn	2 tbsp.	30 ml
Salt	1 tbsp.	15 ml

Toast bread slices and rub the top of each with half a garlic clove. Sprinkle each slice with oil, pepper and salt.

Makes 4 servings.

Panzanella
Toasted Bread with Fresh Tomatoes

This appetizer is best served right away before the bread gets soggy.

Italian bread slices, about 1 inch (2.5 cm) thick	8	8
Tomatoes, finely diced	3	3
Red or green pepper, cored and chopped	1	1
Garlic cloves, finely minced	3	3
Green onions, chopped	2	2
Olive oil	3/4 cup	180 ml
Wine vinegar	2 tbsp.	30 ml
Fresh basil leaves, chopped	2 tbsp.	30 ml
Dried oregano	1 tbsp.	15 ml
Salt and pepper		

Toast bread slices and set aside. Toss remaining ingredients in a large bowl until well incorporated.

Tip: If you are going to be entertaining, this mixture can be prepared and refrigerated one or two days in advance. When ready to serve, divide mixture evenly on bread slices and eat while the bread is still crisp.

Makes 4 servings.

Antipasto Misto
Mixed Appetizer

Head of radicchio, shredded	1	1
Prosciutto slices	8	8
Salami slices	8	8
Capocollo slices	8	8
Zucchini slices, grilled	8	8
Provolone cheese slices	8	8
Green and black olives	1 cup	250 ml
Pickled mixed vegetables	2 cups	500 ml
Olive oil (optional)		

Spread the shredded radicchio so that it covers a large serving platter. Arrange the remaining ingredients on top of the lettuce to make an attractive presentation. If desired, sprinkle some olive oil over the platter and serve immediately.

Serves 4 to 6 people.

Antipasto di Mare
Seafood Platter

Cuttlefish is closely related to squid and may be substituted with squid or octopus if you have trouble finding it.

Squid, small	1 lb.	450 g
Cuttlefish, small	1 lb.	450 g
Scallops, medium	1 lb.	450 g
Shrimp, medium	1 lb.	450 g
Red pepper, seeded and julienned	1	1
Medium onion, chopped	1	1
Fresh fennel, shredded	1	1
Olive oil	3/4 cup	180 ml
Vegetable oil	2 tbsp.	30 ml
White vinegar	1/2 cup	120 ml
Lemon juice	1/2 cup	120 ml
Chili pepper	1 tsp.	5 ml
Fresh parsley, chopped		
Salt and pepper to taste		

Bring a large pot of unsalted water to a boil. Add squid and cuttlefish and cook for 6 to 8 minutes. Then add scallops and shrimps and cook until shrimps turn pink. Drain fish in colander and run under cold water until cool. Peel and de-vein the shrimp and cut fish into bite size pieces. Toss fish with remaining ingredients until well coated. Serve cold, garnished with tomato and cucumber slices and arranged around a platter.

Serves 4 to 6 people.

Antipasto di Gamberoni
Shrimp Platter

Jumbo shrimp (about 32-40)	2 lbs.	900 g
Olive oil	1/4 cup	60 ml
Lemon juice	1/2 cup	120 ml
Balsamic vinegar	1/2 cup	120 ml
Tomato, diced	1	1
Garlic cloves, minced	3	3
Fresh chili pepper	1 tbsp.	15 ml
Salt and pepper		
Head of lettuce, shredded	1	1
Fresh fennel, julienned	1	1
Avocado, peeled and wedged	1	1
Fresh basil or parsley (optional)		

Bring a pot of unsalted water to a boil. Cook shrimp for 5 to 8 minutes, or until they turn pink. Drain and rinse under cold water until cool. Peel and de-vein. In a large bowl, toss together shrimp, oil, lemon juice, balsamic vinegar, tomato, garlic, chili pepper, salt and pepper until well incorporated. Arrange lettuce and fennel on a serving platter and top with the shrimp mixture. Garnish with avocado slices and basil or parsley, if desired, and serve cold.

Serves 4 to 6 people.

Antipasto di Cozze Vino e Pomodoro
Mussels in Wine and Tomato Sauce

Fresh mussels	4 lbs.	1.8 kg
Olive or vegetable oil	1/4 cup	60 ml
Garlic cloves, minced	6	6
Onion, chopped	1	1
Tomato, chopped	2 cups	500 ml
Green onions, chopped	4	4
White wine	1 cup	250 ml
Tomato paste	2 tbsp.	30 ml
Fresh parsley, chopped		
Salt and pepper		

Wash mussels one by one in cold water; set aside. In a large skillet, heat oil and add all ingredients except mussels. Cook for about 8 minutes over medium heat. Add mussels, cover with lid, and cook until mussel shells open.

Tip: Do not overcook or mussels will be the consistency of rubber! Serve immediately on a hot plate or in a large bowl.

Serves 4 to 6 people.

Lumache Mercante di Vino con Funghi
Snails in Red Wine and Mushroom Sauce

Large snails, drained	4 dozen	4 dozen
Butter	1/2 cup	120 ml
Olive oil	1/4 cup	60 ml
Garlic, finely chopped	1/2 cup	120 ml
Shallots, chopped	1/2 cup	120 ml
Flour	2 tbsp.	30 ml
Tomato paste	1 tbsp.	15 ml
Mushrooms, sliced	2 cups	500 ml
Beef broth (see recipe, p. 42)	1 cup	250 ml
Red wine	1 cup	250 ml
Chili pepper preserve (see recipe, p. 18)	1 tbsp.	15 ml

In a saucepan, heat butter and oil and sauté garlic and shallots for 2 minutes. Stir in flour and tomato paste. Add mushrooms and cook for 3 minutes, stirring frequently. Add snails and remaining ingredients and simmer over moderate heat for 6 minutes. Serve with toasted bread.

Makes 60 small appetizers

Antipasto di Salmone Affumicato
Smoked Salmon Platter

Head of lettuce, julienned	1	1
Smoked salmon, thinly sliced	2 lbs.	900 g
Celery heart, wedged	1	1
Roasted green pepper, julienned	1	1
Red onion, finely sliced	1	1
Cucumber, peeled and sliced	1	1

Dressing:

Olive oil	1/2 cup	120 ml
White wine vinegar	1/2 cup	120 ml
Capers	2 tbsp.	30 ml
Dry mustard	1 tbsp.	15 ml
Juice of 3 lemons		
Salt and crushed peppercorn		
Green onion, chopped (optional)		

Arrange the lettuce on a large serving platter. Place salmon slices in the middle and surround with slices of celery, peppers, onions, and cucumbers. Combine oil, vinegar, capers, mustard, lemon juice, salt and pepper and pour dressing over platter. Garnish with green onion, if desired.

Serves 4 people.

Antipasto di Fichi e Prosciutto
Fresh Fig and Prosciutto Appetizer

Prosciutto slices	24	24
Fresh figs, peeled	24	24
Oranges, peeled and sliced	2	2
Lemons, wedged	2	2
Stuffed olives	1 cup	250 ml
Olive oil	1/2 cup	120 ml
Whole walnuts (optional)	1/3 cup	90 ml

Wrap each fig in one prosciutto slice to make 24 individual appetizers. Arrange on a large serving platter with orange and lemon wedges, and olives. Keep refrigerated until ready to use, then drizzle with olive oil and add walnuts, if desired.

Serves 4 to 6 people.

Antipasto di Vegetali
Vegetable Platter

Medium eggplant, peeled and sliced 1/2 inch (1 cm) thick	1	1
Zucchini, washed and sliced 1 inch (2.5 cm) thick	2	2
Large Cremini mushrooms	12	12
Large Spanish onion, sliced 1 inch (2.5 cm) thick	1	1
Red peppers	4	4
Head of radicchio, quartered	1	1
Olive oil	1/2 cup	120 ml
Wine or balsamic vinegar	1/3 cup	90 ml
Garlic cloves, minced	3	3
Dried basil	1 tbsp.	15 ml
Salt and pepper		

On a hot grill, cook the eggplant, zucchini, mushrooms, and onion until golden brown on both sides. Set aside to cool. To roast peppers, place on grill and cook until skin turns almost black. Remove from heat and run under cold water to remove skin; seed and julienne. Arrange vegetables on a large serving platter with radicchio. Whisk together oil, vinegar, garlic, basil, salt and pepper and pour over vegetables.

Serves 4 people.

Soups and Broth

Soup, or *zuppa*, is normally served as the *primo piatto*, or first course of a meal. If a soup is hearty enough, though, it can even be served as the main course.

Soup is so versatile it can be served at any time of the day. It can be clear like broth (*brodo, minestrina*), it can be creamed or puréed (*crema*), thickened with pasta, rice, or beans (*minestra*), with vegetables and meat (*minestrone*), or it can even be poured over pieces of roasted bread (*zuppa*). It is an economical dish, allowing you to use up scraps of vegetables or meat bones that you would otherwise have discarded.

And, of course, it is healthy. Not only does it provide all sorts of nutrients, but it also cleans out your system and fills you up without filling you out.

When you are making soup, especially stock or broth, it is a good idea to make more than you need and freeze the rest for later use. Soup can be stored in the freezer for 3 months. Thaw it overnight in the refrigerator and adjust the seasonings and consistency when you reheat it.

Brodo di Pollo
Chicken Broth

Chicken bones	3 lbs.	1.4 kg
Water	8 quarts	8 litres
The peel of 5 to 8 carrots		
Onion, quartered	1	1
Head of garlic, sliced	1	1
Celery greens	1 bunch	1 bunch
Parsley stems	1 bunch	1 bunch
Peppercorn	3 tbsp.	50 ml
Dried sage	1 tbsp.	15 ml
Bay leaves, crumbled	2	2
Cinnamon	1 stick	1 stick
Salt, to taste		

Combine all ingredients in a large stockpot and bring to a boil over high heat. Once it boils, reduce the heat to medium and begin skimming the broth. Continue to simmer for at least 40 minutes or until the broth reduces by half. Strain through a sieve and serve.

You may keep this broth in the refrigerator for about a week, or freeze it for later use.

Makes about 16 cups/4 litres.

Variation: Chicken Stock

In a large stockpot, melt 1 cup (250 ml) of butter. Add all ingredients except water, and sauté until golden brown. Add water and simmer until stock is reduced by half. Strain through a sieve and serve.

This stock may also be stored in the refrigerator and used later for making a demiglace or for gravy.

Brodo di Tacchino
Turkey Broth

Turkey bones	3 lbs.	1.4 kg
Water	8 quarts	8 litres
The peel of 10 carrots		
Celery stalks, chopped	4	4
Shallots, quartered	4	4
Garlic cloves, halved	6	6
The cores of 2 to 4 red peppers		
The peel of 2 oranges		
Parsley stems	1 bunch	1 bunch
Dried rosemary	1 tbsp.	15 ml
Ginger powder	1 tbsp.	15 ml
Bay leaves, crumbled	4	4
White peppercorn	3 tbsp.	50 ml
Salt, to taste		

Combine all ingredients in a large stockpot and bring to a boil over high heat. Once it boils, reduce heat to medium and skim the broth. Continue cooking for at least 40 minutes, or until broth reduces by half. Strain through a sieve and serve.

This broth may be stored in the refrigerator for about 1 week or frozen for later use.

Makes about 16 cups/4 litres.

Variation: Turkey Stock

In a large stockpot, melt 1 cup (250 ml) of butter. Add all ingredients except water and sauté until golden brown. Add water and simmer until stock is reduced by half. Strain through a sieve and serve.

This stock may also be stored in the refrigerator or frozen for later use.

"Singing and cooking are the same.
They both give us a chance to find
happiness in creativity."

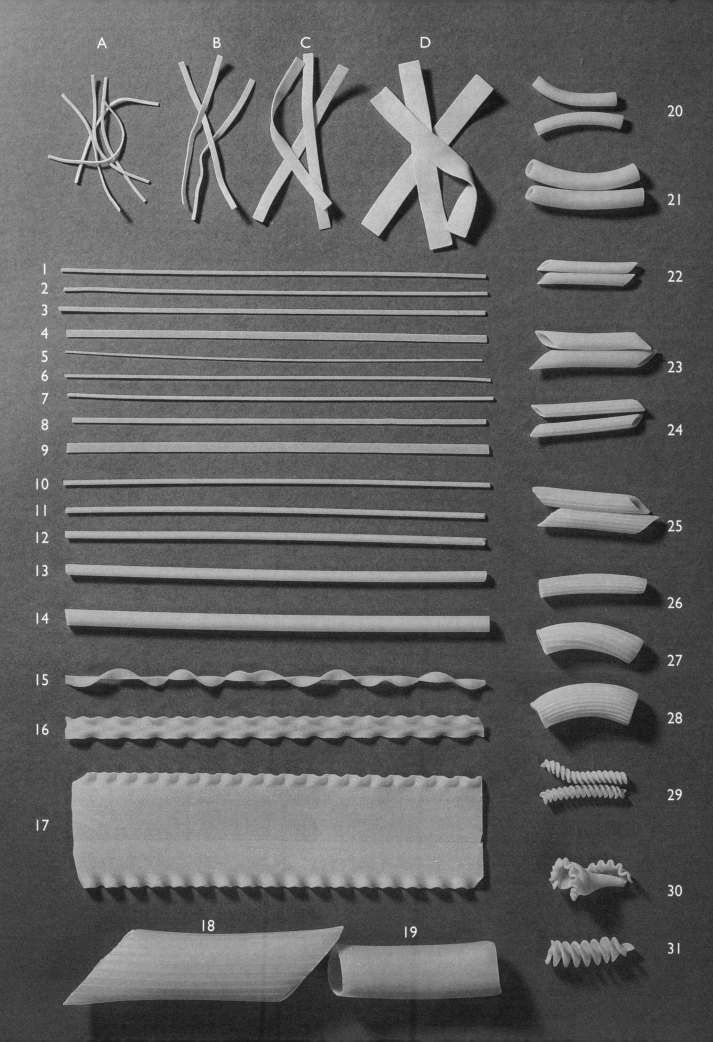

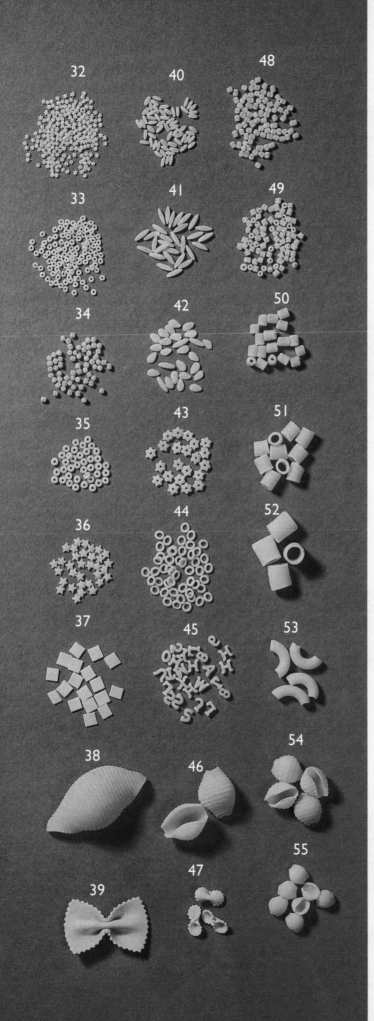

Macaroni Styles

A. Fini (fine)
B. Médie (medium)
C. Larghe (broad)
D. Extra Larghe (extra broad)
1. Egg Spaghettini
2. Egg Spaghetti
3. Egg Tagliatellini
4. Egg Tagliatelle
5. Vermicelli
6. Spaghettini (thin spaghetti)
7. Spaghetti
8. Linguine (flat spaghetti)
9. Fettuccini
10. Bucatini
11. Perciatelli (thin macaroni)
12. Maccaroncelli (macaroni)
13. Mezzani (medium macaroni)
14. Ziti (large macaroni)
15. Yolanda
16. Mafalda
17. Lasagna
18. Manicotti
19. Tufoli
20. Mezzani Tagliati (cut macaroni, medium)
21. Ziti Tagliati (cut macaroni, large)
22. Pennine (small pens)
23. Penne Lisce (pens)
24. Pennine Rigate (small ribbed pens)
25. Penne Rigate (ribbed pens)
26. Magliette Rigate (cut ribbed macaroni)
27. Bocconcini (half rigatoni)
28. Rigatoni (large ribbed elbows)
29. Fusilli (springs)
30. Fiori (flowers)
31. Rotini (turrets)
32. Egg Pastina
33. Pastina
34. Egg Barley
35. Egg Rings
36. Egg Stars
37. Egg Squares
38. Lumaconi (jumbo shells)
39. Galle (bow ties)
40. Risini (rice)
41. Orzo (oats)
42. Semi Mellone (melon seeds)
43. Stelline (stars)
44. Anellini (rings)
45. Alfabeti (alphabets)
46. Lumache (large shells)
47. Tripolini (bow ties No. 1)
48. Acini Peppe (lead shots)
49. Pepe Bucato (beads)
50. Tubettini (small cut macaroni)
51. Tubetti (medium cut macaroni)
52. Ditali (large cut macaroni)
53. Stivaletti (ready cut)
54. Conchiglie (medium shells)
55. Lumachine (baby shells)

Erbe Aromatica Top row: (L to R) Oregano, Sage, Basil, Tarragon   Bottom Row: (L to R) Mint, Thyme, Chives, Italian parsley, Dill

Brodo di Pesce
Fish Broth

The head and bones of one salmon, halibut, or snapper	3 to 4 lbs.	1.5 kg (approx.)
Water	4 quarts	4 litres
Vegetable or olive oil	1/2 cup	120 ml
Celery stalks, diced	2	2
The peel of 8 carrots		
Onion, quartered	1	1
Garlic cloves, crushed	4	4
Parsley stems	1 bunch	1 bunch
The peel of 2 lemons		
The cores of 4 red peppers		
Dried thyme	1 tbsp.	15 ml
Peppercorn	3 tbsp.	50 ml
Salt, to taste		

Combine all ingredients in a large stockpot and bring to a boil over high heat. Once it boils, reduce heat to medium and skim the broth. Simmer for about 2 hours, stirring occasionally. Strain through a sieve and serve. This can be refrigerated for up to two weeks.

Makes about 12 cups/3 litres.

Variation: Fish Stock

In a large stockpot, heat oil. Add all ingredients except water and sauté until golden brown. Add water and lower heat to medium. Simmer until stock is reduced by half. Strain through a sieve and serve. This stock may also be stored in the refrigerator.

Brodo di Manzo
Beef Broth

Olive oil	1/4 cup	60 ml
Beef bones	4 lbs.	1.8 kg
Onions, diced with skins	4	4
Garlic cloves, pressed	3	3
Celery stalks, diced	6	6
Peels of 6 carrots		
Fresh ginger root, sliced	1/4 cup	60 ml
Prepared horseradish	1 tbsp.	15 ml
Fresh parsley, chopped	1 bunch	1 bunch
Dried rosemary	2 tbsp.	30 ml
Bay leaves, crushed	6	6
Peppercorn, crushed	1/4 cup	60 ml
Tomato paste	2 tbsp.	30 ml
Salt (optional)	1 tbsp.	15 ml
Water	6 quarts	6 litres
Red wine (optional)	1 cup	250 ml

In a large stockpot, heat the oil and sauté all the ingredients except the water and wine for 10 minutes, stirring frequently. Add in the water and wine and bring to a boil. Lower the heat to medium and simmer for 2 hours, stirring occasionally, until the liquid reduces by half. Strain the broth into jars and let cool. You may store the broth in the refrigerator or freezer for future use.

Makes about 12 cups/3 litres.

Brodo di Vegetali
Vegetable Stock

Vegetable oil	1/4 cup	60 ml
Carrot peels	2 cups	500 ml
Celery stalks and tops, diced	4 cups	1 litre
Onions, diced with skins	4	4
Tomatoes, chopped	4	4

Bell pepper cores	4–6	4–6
Lettuce cores	4–6	4–6
Garlic cloves, pressed	4	4
Fresh parsley stems, chopped	2 bunches	2 bunches
Bay leaves, crushed	6	6
Peppercorn	2 tbsp.	30 ml
Salt	1 tbsp.	15 ml
Water	6 quarts	6 litres
White wine (optional)	1 cup	250 ml

In a large stockpot, heat the oil and add in all the ingredients except the water and wine. Stir over medium heat for about 15 minutes, or until the vegetables have browned. Add in the water and wine and simmer about 2 hours, or until the liquid reduces by half. Strain the stock into jars and store it in the refrigerator or freezer for future use.

Makes about 12 cups/3 litres.

Brodo Ristretto di Manzo
Beef Stock

Beef bones	6 lbs.	2.7 kg
Water	8 quarts	8 litres
Vegetable oil	1/4 cup	60 ml
Carrots, diced	2	2
Celery stalks, coarsely chopped	4	4
Onions, quartered	2	2
Garlic cloves, crushed	6	6
Tomato paste	1/4 cup	60 ml
or 6 ripe tomatoes, chopped		
Peppercorn, crushed	1/4 cup	60 ml
Bay leaves, crumbled	4	4
Salt, to taste		

Heat oil in a large stockpot. Add all ingredients except water and sauté until brown, stirring frequently. Add water and bring to a boil. Lower heat and skim the broth. Cover and simmer for 2 to 3 hours. Strain through a sieve and serve.

You may store in the refrigerator for one week or freeze for later use.

Makes about 16 cups/4 litres.

Zuppa di Riso e Patate
Rice and Potato Soup

Oil	3 tbsp.	50 ml
Onion, chopped	1	1
Garlic clove, minced	1	1
Pancetta, chopped	4 oz.	115 g
Celery stalk, chopped	1	1
Carrot, diced	1	1
Potatoes, peeled and diced	2	2
Chicken broth (see recipe, p. 39)	2 quarts	2 litres
Rice, rinsed	1 cup	250 ml
Parmesan or Romano cheese	3 tbsp.	50 ml
Parsley, chopped, to taste		
Salt and pepper, to taste		

In a medium saucepan, heat oil and sauté onion, garlic, pancetta, celery, carrot, and potatoes until golden brown. Add broth and bring to a boil. Add rice and simmer for 20 to 25 minutes, stirring occasionally, until rice is tender. Mix in grated cheese, parsley, salt and pepper. Serve immediately.

Makes 4 servings.

Minestra di Pasta e Patate
Pasta and Potato Soup

Chicken broth (see recipe, p. 39)	2 quarts	2 litres
Elbow or any short pasta	1 cup	250 ml
Olive oil	2 tbsp.	30 ml
Pancetta or ham, chopped	4 oz.	115 g
Onion or leek, chopped	1	1
Garlic clove, minced	1	1
Green pepper, chopped	1	1
Potatoes, peeled and diced	2	2
Parmesan cheese, grated	3 tbsp.	50 ml
Dried basil or marjoram	1 pinch	1 pinch
Chopped parsley, to taste		
Salt and pepper, to taste		

Bring chicken broth to a boil in a medium saucepan. Add pasta and stir occasionally. In a fry pan, heat oil and sauté pancetta, onion, garlic, green pepper and potatoes until tender. Add sautéed vegetables to broth and simmer until pasta is tender. Mix in cheese, basil or marjoram, parsley, salt and pepper.

Makes 4 servings.

Minestrone
Vegetable Soup with Beef

This recipe was invented to use up the bones from a roast. The meat should be cut away from the bones and diced, but the bones should not be thrown away until all the goodness has been taken from them in the cooking. If you don't have any leftover meat or bones, you can still cook the soup with fresh meat.

Olive oil	1/2 cup	120 ml
Red or white onion, chopped	1 medium	1 medium
Leek, chopped	1	1
Green onions, chopped	2	2
Celery stalks, chopped	2	
Cabbage, shredded	1/4 head	
Tomato, chopped	1	1
Salt and pepper, to taste		
Beef, diced, and bones from roast	6 oz.	170 g
Tomato paste	1 tbsp.	15 ml
Beef stock (see recipe, p. 43)	4 cups	1 litre
Fusilli pasta	1 1/2 cups	750 ml

Heat the oil in a soup pot and sauté the next 7 ingredients for 5 to 10 minutes. Add the tomato paste and beef stock and cook on medium heat for about 15 minutes. Meanwhile, cook the pasta. Add to the soup and simmer for 20 minutes. Remove the bones from the soup and serve.

Serves 4 to 6

Pasta e Fagioli
Pasta and Bean Soup

Ditali are short, tube-shaped macaroni used mainly for soup.

Ingredient	Imperial	Metric
Olive oil	3 tbsp.	50 ml
Onion, chopped	1	1
Garlic clove, minced	1	1
Celery stalk, diced	1	1
Pancetta, chopped	4 oz.	115 g
Chicken broth (see recipe, p. 39)	2 quarts	2 litres
Tomatoes, peeled or strained	1 cup	250 ml
Ditali or elbow macaroni	1 cup	250 ml
Romano beans, drained	19 fl. oz.	540 ml
Chili pepper	1 pinch	1 pinch
Chopped parsley, to taste		
Salt and pepper, to taste		

In a medium saucepan, heat oil and sauté onion, garlic, celery, and pancetta until slightly browned. Add the broth and tomatoes and bring to a boil. Add pasta and remaining ingredients, stirring frequently. Simmer until pasta is tender. Serve with some grated cheese, if preferred.

Makes 4 servings.

Zuppa di Ceci e Pasta
Pasta and Chickpea Soup

Ingredient	Imperial	Metric
Chicken broth (see recipe, p. 39)	1 1/2 quarts	1.5 litres
Short pasta	2 cups	500 ml
Tomatoes, strained	1/2 cup	120 ml
Chickpeas, drained	19 fl. oz.	540 ml
Olive oil	2 tbsp.	30 ml
Onion, chopped	1	1
Garlic cloves, minced	2	2
Pancetta, chopped	4 oz.	115 g
Anchovy fillets	2	2
Dried rosemary	1 pinch	1 pinch
Chopped parsley, to taste		

Salt and pepper, to taste

In a medium saucepan, bring broth to a boil. Add pasta, tomatoes, and chickpeas. In a fry pan, heat oil and sauté onion, garlic, pancetta, and anchovy for 6 to 8 minutes, until tender. Stir into broth and continue to simmer until pasta is tender. Sprinkle in rosemary, parsley, salt and pepper. Serve with grated Parmesan cheese, if preferred.

Makes 4 servings.

Zuppa di Fave, Pancetta e Pasta
Fava Bean Soup with Pancetta and Pasta

Olive oil	2 tbsp.	30 ml
Onion, chopped	1	1
Garlic clove, minced	1	1
Pancetta, chopped	4 oz.	115 g
Celery stalk, chopped	1	1
Red or green pepper, diced	1/2	1/2
Chicken broth (see recipe, p. 39)	2 quarts	2 litres
Small pasta	1 cup	250 ml
Fava beans, drained	19 fl. oz.	540 ml
Chili pepper	1 pinch	
Salt and pepper, to taste		
Chopped parsley, to taste		
Grated Parmesan cheese	3 tbsp.	50 ml

In a medium saucepan, heat oil and sauté onion, garlic, pancetta, celery, and pepper for 3 to 5 minutes, stirring frequently. Add the broth and bring to a boil. Add remaining ingredients, except cheese, and continue to simmer for 10 to 16 minutes, stirring occasionally, until pasta is tender. Sprinkle with more parsley and grated cheese, if preferred.

Makes 4 servings.

Zuppa di Broccoli
Cream of Broccoli Soup

Butter	2 tbsp.	30 ml
Olive oil or bacon fat	2 tbsp.	30 ml
Onion, chopped	1	1
Garlic clove, minced	1	1
Red pepper, diced	1/2	1/2
Broccoli, peeled and chopped	1 bunch	1 bunch
Flour	1 tbsp.	15 ml
Chicken broth (see recipe, p. 39)	2 quarts	2 litres
35% cream	3/4 cup	180 ml
(or 1 cup/250 ml of boiling milk)		
Nutmeg, grated	1 pinch	1 pinch
Chopped parsley, to taste		
Salt and pepper, to taste		

In a medium saucepan, heat butter and oil and sauté onion, garlic, red pepper, and broccoli until tender. Stir in flour, making sure vegetables are well coated. Add broth and remaining ingredients and bring to a boil. Simmer for 8 to 10 minutes over medium heat, stirring frequently. Serve with grated cheese, if preferred.

Makes 4 servings.

Zuppa di Spinaci
Cream of Spinach Soup

Spinach, washed, cooked and chopped	1 bunch	1 bunch
Butter	3 tbsp.	50 ml
Onion, chopped	1	1
Flour	2 tbsp.	30 ml
Chicken broth (see recipe, p. 39)	2 quarts	2 litres
35% cream or boiling milk	2 cups	500 ml
Fresh parsley, chopped	2 tbsp.	30 ml
Nutmeg, grated	1/2 tsp.	2 ml
Salt and pepper, to taste		

In a medium saucepan, heat butter and sauté onion until light brown. Stir in flour.

Add remaining ingredients and bring to a boil. Simmer for 15 minutes over moderate heat, stirring occasionally. Serve with croutons, if preferred.

Makes 4 servings.

Zuppa di Vongole e Crema
Cream of Clam Soup

Butter	2 tbsp.	30 ml
Oil	3 tbsp.	50 ml
Onion, chopped	1	1
(or the white part of 2 Leeks)		
Garlic clove, minced	1	1
Celery stalk, chopped	1	1
Carrot, diced	1	1
Flour	2 tbsp.	30 ml
Fish or chicken broth	1 1/2 quarts	1.5 litres
(see recipes, p. 41/39)		
10% cream, boiling	2 cups	500 ml
White wine (optional)	1/2 cup	120 ml
Tin of clams, drained	5 oz	142 g
Chopped parsley, to taste		
Salt and pepper, to taste		

In a medium saucepan, heat butter and oil. Sauté onion, garlic, celery and carrots until transparent. Stir in flour. Add the broth and bring to a boil. Simmer for 6 to 8 minutes, stirring frequently. Add remaining ingredients and simmer for an additional 5 minutes.

Makes 4 servings.

Minestra di Gran Turco
Cornmeal Soup

Vegetable oil	1/4 cup	60 ml
Onion, chopped	1/2 cup	120 ml
Celery, chopped	1/2 cup	120 ml
Red or green pepper, chopped	1/2 cup	120 ml
Carrots, chopped	1/2 cup	120 ml
Frozen peas	1 cup	250 ml
Garlic, minced	1 tbsp.	15 ml
Chicken broth (see recipe, p. 39)	1 quart	1 litre
Tomato paste	2 tbsp.	30 ml
Cooking wine	1/2 cup	120 ml
Aromatic preserve (see recipe, p. 17)	1 tbsp.	15 ml
Chili pepper preserve (see recipe, p. 18)	1 tbsp.	15 ml
Water	1 cup	250 ml
Cornmeal	1/2 cup	120 ml
Salt and crushed peppercorn, to taste		

In a large saucepan, heat oil and sauté all the vegetables for 3 to 5 minutes, stirring occasionally. Add chicken broth, tomato paste, wine and condiments and bring to a boil, stirring well. In a separate bowl, dilute the cornmeal with water and add to the soup. Lower heat to medium and simmer for 20 minutes, stirring frequently. Season with salt and pepper and serve.

Makes 4 to 6 servings.

Zuppa di Pollo con Vegetali
Chicken Vegetable Soup

Olive oil	3 tbsp.	50 ml
Onion, chopped	1	1
Garlic clove, minced	1	1
Carrot, diced	1	1
Celery stalk, diced	1	1
Chicken breast, skinned and diced	1	1
Chicken broth (see recipe, p. 39)	2 quarts	2 litres
Tomato, chopped	1	1

Red pepper, chopped	1/2	1/2
Saffron	1 pinch	1 pinch
Cinnamon	1 pinch	1 pinch
Parsley, chopped, to taste		
Salt and pepper, to taste		

In a medium saucepan, heat oil over high heat and sauté onion, carrot, celery, garlic, and chicken for 4 to 6 minutes, stirring frequently. Add remaining ingredients and simmer for 20 to 25 minutes, stirring occasionally, until vegetables are tender. Serve hot, sprinkled with grated cheese, if preferred.

Makes 4 servings.

Minestra di Lenticchie e Vegetali
Lentil and Vegetable Soup

Pancetta is Italian cured bacon.

Chicken broth (see recipe, p. 39)	2 quarts	2 litres
Canned lentils, drained	19 fl. oz.	540 ml
Tomatoes, peeled or strained	1 cup	250 ml
Olive oil	3 tbsp.	50 ml
Onion, chopped	1	1
Garlic clove, minced	1	1
Pancetta or bacon, chopped	4 oz.	115 g
Celery stalk, chopped	1	1
Carrot, diced	1	1
Potato, peeled and diced	1	1
Parsley, chopped, to taste		
Salt and pepper, to taste		

In a medium saucepan, bring chicken broth to a boil. Add lentils and tomatoes. In a fry pan, heat oil over medium heat and sauté remaining ingredients until tender. Add sautéed vegetables to broth and continue to simmer for another 10 minutes. Serve hot, sprinkled with some chili pepper, if preferred.

Makes 4 servings.

Rice and Grains

Besides soup and pasta, other dishes to serve as a first course are risotto, gnocchi, polenta or pizza.

Risotto has long been a staple in northern Italian cooking. Rice was first cultivated in Italy on the Lombardy plain and in the Po Valley in the 15th century. Since then, the variety of ways to prepare rice has made it an indispensable part of Italian cuisine. Risotto ("little rice") has a creamy consistency and is generally made from Arborio (Italian short grain) rice, which is cooked in stock with various seasonings. If you prefer other types of rice (*riso*), these recipes include some nice pilafs using long-grain white rice, for which you can substitute brown or even wild rice.

Gnocchi are small Italian dumplings made either from potatoes, a version popular in the North, or from semolina, which is popular in the South. They can be boiled, baked, or even grilled.

Polenta or cooked cornmeal is another popular dish of northern Italy. Originally, the northern Italians, who live in areas rich with chestnut trees, used chestnut flour to make their polenta. But now this thick dish is made primarily with coarse cornmeal and cooked to a desired consistency. It can be served as a porridge, or baked and grilled and then sliced.

Pizza is a flat yeast bread topped with various ingredients. Though it has probably been around for thousands of years, it is the version originating in Naples that has made the dish so famous. The traditional *pizza alla Margherita* is topped simply with tomato, mozzarella and basil, and is still the best version around. *Pizza bianca* is topped only with olive oil, garlic and herbs like rosemary and black pepper, and sometimes with anchovies.

Risotto in Padella alla Forestiere

Rice Pilaf Foreigner Style

Long-grain rice	1 1/2 cups	375 ml
Olive oil	5 tbsp.	75 ml
Butter or margarine	3 tbsp.	50 ml
Red onion, chopped	1	1
Garlic cloves, minced	4	4
Portobello mushrooms, sliced	3 cups	750 ml
Red or green pepper, diced	2	2
Tomato purée	2 cups	500 ml
Chicken broth (see recipe, p. 39)	1 cup	250 ml
White wine	1/2 cup	120 ml
Salt and pepper, to taste		

Bring a pot of salted water to a boil. Add rice and simmer over medium heat for 25 to 30 minutes, stirring occasionally until rice is tender. In a large fry pan, heat oil and butter and sauté onion, garlic, mushrooms, and peppers until tender. Add remaining ingredients and simmer over medium heat for about 25 minutes. Add the drained rice and mix until well coated.

Makes 4 servings.

Risotto con Gamberi e Crema
Rice with Shrimp and Cream Sauce

Arborio rice	1 1/2 cups	375 ml
Olive oil	1/4 cup	60 ml
Onion, chopped	1/2	1/2
Mushrooms, sliced	6	6
Red pepper, diced	1/2	1/2
Asparagus stalks, chopped	4	4
Shrimp, medium sized, peeled and de-veined	2 cups	480 ml
Chicken broth (see recipe, p. 39)	3/4 cup	180 ml
35% cream	1/2 cup	120 ml
White wine (optional)	1/2 cup	120 ml
Flour	1 tbsp.	15 ml
Nutmeg	1 pinch	1 pinch
Basil	1 pinch	1 pinch
Chopped parsley, to taste		
Salt and pepper, to taste		
Parmesan cheese	1/3 cup	90 ml

In a medium saucepan, combine rice and 1 cup (250 ml) of water. Bring to a boil and simmer for 18 minutes, adding additional water 1/2 cup (120 ml) at a time until rice is tender. In a large fry pan, heat oil and sauté onion, mushrooms, red pepper, and asparagus until lightly browned. Add remaining ingredients, except cheese, and bring to a boil. Simmer for 10 to 12 minutes, stirring occasionally. Add the cooked rice and cheese and stir until well incorporated. Let it rest 2 to 3 minutes before serving.

Makes 4 servings.

Risotto con Conserva di Pomodori Secchi e Porcini
Rice with Sun-Dried Tomato and Porcini Mushroom Preserve

Arborio rice	1 1/2 cups	375 ml
Butter	1/4 cup	60 ml
Green onion, chopped	1 cup	250 ml
Sun-dried tomato preserve (see recipe, p. 21)	1/4 cup	60 ml

Porcini mushroom preserve (see recipe, p. 22)	1/4 cup	60 ml
Chili pepper preserve (see recipe, p. 18)	1 tbsp.	15 ml
Chicken broth (see recipe, p. 39)	3/4 cup	180 ml
White wine	1/2 cup	120 ml
10% cream, boiled	1 cup	250 ml
Salt and pepper, to taste		

In a medium saucepan, combine rice and 1 cup (250 ml) of water. Bring to a boil and cook for 18 minutes, adding additional water 1/2 cup (120 ml) at a time until rice is tender. In a large fry pan, heat butter and sauté green onion for 4 minutes, stirring frequently. Add remaining ingredients and lower heat to medium. Simmer for 8 to 10 minutes, stirring frequently. Stir in the cooked rice and simmer in the sauce for a few minutes before serving. Place rice on a platter and garnish with an assortment of vegetables. Top with some grated Parmesan, if desired.

Makes 4 servings.

Risotto in Padella con Asparagi e Funghi
Rice Pilaf with Asparagus and Mushroom

Arborio rice	1 1/2 cups	375 ml
Vegetable oil	5 tbsp.	75 ml
Unsalted butter	2 tbsp.	30 ml
Onion, chopped	1	1
Mushrooms, sliced	2 cups	500 ml
Asparagus, peeled and chopped	2 cups	500 ml
Red pepper, julienned	1/2	1/2
Chicken broth (see recipe, p. 39)	1 1/2 cups	375 ml
Lemon juice	1/4 cup	60 ml
Romano cheese, grated	1 cup	250 ml
Parsley, chopped	1/2 cup	120 ml
Salt and pepper, to taste		

Bring a pot of salted water to a boil. Add rice and simmer over medium heat for 18 minutes, stirring occasionally until rice is tender. In a large skillet, heat oil and butter and sauté onion, mushroom, asparagus, and pepper until lightly browned. Add the broth, lemon juice, parsley, salt and pepper and simmer over medium heat. Add the drained rice and cheese and stir until well coated.

Makes 4 servings.

Risi e Bisi in Padella
Rice and Pea Casserole

Arborio rice	1 1/2 cups	375 ml
Vegetable oil	1/3 cup	90 ml
Butter	2 tbsp.	30 ml
Onion, chopped	1	1
Red pepper, cored and chopped	1	1
Pancetta or bacon	1 cup	250 ml
Frozen peas	2 cups	500 ml
Chicken broth (see recipe, p. 39)	1 1/4 cups	310 ml
Lemon juice	1/2 cup	120 ml
Parsley, chopped	1/2 cup	120 ml
Salt and pepper, to taste		

Bring a pot of salted water to a boil. Add rice and simmer for 18 minutes, stirring occasionally until tender. In a large skillet or Dutch oven, heat oil and butter and sauté onion and pepper until translucent. Add pancetta and continue to sauté for 3 to 5 minutes. Add remaining ingredients and simmer until peas are cooked through. Add the drained rice and mix until well coated.

Makes 4 servings.

Frittelle di Riso
Fried Rice Balls

Arborio rice	1 cup	250 ml
Eggs	6	6
10% cream or milk	1/2 cup	120 ml
Bread crumbs	2 cups	500 ml
All-purpose flour	3 tbsp.	50 ml
Parmesan cheese, grated	1/2 cup	120 ml
Parsley, chopped	1/2 cup	120 ml
Dried basil	1 tbsp.	15 ml
Baking powder	1 tsp.	5 ml
Salt and pepper, to taste		
Vegetable oil, for frying	1 cup	250 ml

Bring a pot of salted water to a boil. Add rice and simmer for 18 minutes, stirring occasionally until rice is tender. Drain and allow to cool in a large bowl. Add all ingredients except oil to the cooled rice and mix thoroughly. Form the mixture into balls, about 1/3 cup (85 ml) for each one, and flatten into hamburger-sized rounds, about 1 inch (2.5 cm) thick. In a large skillet, heat 1/2 cup (120 ml) of the oil until it reaches a temperature of 300°F (150°C). Fry the rice balls for 2 minutes on each side, or until golden brown. Add remaining oil as necessary. Keep the fried rice balls warm as you continue to fry the remaining batch.

Makes about 10 to 12 large rice balls

Gnocchi
Potato Dumplings

Potatoes	4 lbs.	1.8 kg
Eggs	5	5
All-purpose flour	2 cups	500 ml
Nutmeg, grated	1 tsp.	5 ml
Salt and pepper, to taste		
Corn flour, as needed		

Place potatoes in a large pot and cover with water. Boil until tender, about 35 minutes. Drain and rinse under cold water. Peel and mash until smooth. In a large bowl, combine potatoes with eggs, flour, nutmeg, salt and pepper and mix into a stiff dough. Divide the dough into small portions and roll on a lightly floured surface into long snake-like strips. Cut into 1-inch (2.5-cm) lengths and sprinkle with corn flour to prevent sticking. Continue until all the dough is used up. Bring a large pot of salted water to a boil. Add the gnocchi and cook for 5 to 10 minutes, stirring gently. When they bob to the surface, they are ready. Drain and serve with your preferred sauce.

Serves 4 to 6.

Gnocchi al Pomodoro
Gnocchi with Tomato Sauce

Gnocchi (see recipe, p. 57)	2 lbs.	900 g
Olive oil	3 tbsp.	50 ml
Onion, chopped	1	1
Garlic clove, minced	1	1
Pancetta, chopped	4 oz.	115 g
Chicken broth (see recipe, p. 39)	3/4 cup	180 ml
Red or White wine	1/2 cup	120 ml
Tomato purée	1 cup	250 ml
Dried basil	1 tsp.	5 ml
Nutmeg	1 pinch	1 pinch
Chopped parsley, to taste		
Salt and pepper, to taste		
Parmesan or Romano cheese	3 tbsp.	50 ml
Chili pepper, to taste (optional)		

Bring a large pot of salted water to a boil. Add gnocchi and boil for about 10 minutes, or until tender. In a fry pan, heat oil and sauté onion, garlic and pancetta until lightly browned. Add remaining ingredients, except cheese and chili pepper and simmer for 10 to 15 minutes, stirring occasionally. Drain the gnocchi and toss with sauce and grated cheese. Sprinkle with chili pepper, if desired.

Makes 4 servings.

Gnocchi alla Panna
Gnocchi with Cream Sauce

Gnocchi (see recipe, p. 57)	2 lbs.	900 g
Butter	3 tbsp.	50 ml
Green onions, chopped	4	4
Red pepper, diced	1/2	1/2
Cooked ham, diced	1/2 cup	120 ml
Flour	1 tbsp.	15 ml
35% cream or boiling milk	1/2 cup	120 ml
Chicken broth (see recipe, p. 39)	1/2 cup	120 ml
Nutmeg	1 pinch	1 pinch

Basil	1 pinch	1 pinch
Chopped parsley, to taste		
Salt and pepper, to taste		
Parmesan or Romano cheese	1/4 cup	60 ml

Bring a large pot of salted water to a boil. Add gnocchi and boil for about 10 minutes, or until tender. In a fry pan, heat butter and sauté onion, pepper, and ham for 2 to 3 minutes. Stir in flour until well coated. Add remaining ingredients except cheese and simmer for 5 to 7 minutes, or until the sauce reduces a bit. Drain the gnocchi and toss with sauce and grated cheese.

Makes 4 servings.

Polenta
Cornmeal

This recipe may be served directly from the pot as a "soft polenta."

Chicken broth	2 quarts	2 litres
(see recipe, p. 39)		
Cornmeal	3 cups	750 ml
Salt	1 tbsp.	15 ml
Crushed peppercorn	1 tsp.	5 ml

In a medium saucepan, bring 4 cups (1 litre) of the chicken broth to a boil. Mix remaining broth with cornmeal until smooth. Slowly add this mixture into the boiling broth, whisking constantly. Simmer over low heat for 30 to 40 minutes. The longer you cook it, the thicker it will be. Pour the polenta into an oiled sheet pan and cool. Cut into desired shape and serve as a side dish or grill to reheat.

Makes 4 to 6 servings.

Pasta per Pizza
Pizza Dough

This is a large-batch recipe suitable for a party or for freezing.

Warm water	3 1/2 cups	875 ml
Dry yeast	1/4 cup	60 ml
Vegetable oil	1/4 cup	60 ml
Sugar	3 tbsp.	50 ml
Salt	2 tbsp.	30 ml
Egg whites	2	2
All-purpose flour	11 cups	2.75 L

In a large bowl, combine water, yeast, oil, sugar, salt and egg whites. Whisk together until the mixture is foamy. Mix in the flour with a wooden spoon until you are able to handle it by hand. You may have to add in more water or more flour, depending on the consistency. Knead the dough in the bowl until it is soft and smooth. Divide the dough into 8 sections. Place them on a floured surface and cover them with a towel. Let them rise for at least 40 minutes. When the dough has risen, punch it down and knead it for a minute or so. Roll or stretch out each section on a lightly floured surface into 12-inch (30-cm) rounds. (If you are making extra pizzas for freezing, pre-cook them for 4 to 5 minutes. Let them cool and freeze them individually in freezer-proof bags.) Preheat your oven to 425°F (220°C). Grease your 12-inch (30-cm) round pizza pans with a bit of oil and dust with flour. Place the rolled out dough on the pan and top with whatever toppings you desire. Depending on the topping, the cooking time will be about 15 minutes, more or less.

Makes eight 12-inch (30-cm) round pizzas, or four 12 x 18-inch (30 x 45-cm) pizzas.

Plain Pizza

Prepare dough according to above recipe and roll onto pan. To make one pizza, top with 1 cup (250 ml) of pizza sauce (see recipe, p. 29) and 1 1/2 cups (375 ml) of shredded mozzarella cheese. Bake in a pre-heated 450°F (230°C) oven for 17 to 20 minutes, or until the edges are golden.

Pepperoni Pizza

Prepare dough according to above recipe and roll onto pan. To make one pizza, top with 1 cup (250 ml) of pizza sauce (see recipe, p. 29) and 1 1/2 cups (375 ml) of shredded mozzarella or brick cheese, and 1 cup (250 ml) of sliced pepperoni. Bake in a pre-heated 450°F (230°C) oven for 17 to 20 minutes, or until the edges are golden.

Pizza Primavera

Prepare dough according to above recipe and roll onto pan. To make one pizza, top with 1 cup (250 ml) of pizza sauce (see recipe, p. 29), 1 cup (250 ml) of shredded mozzarella, and 1 cup (250 ml) of assorted sliced vegetables like green or red peppers, mushrooms, olives, broccoli, or fresh tomatoes. Bake in a pre-heated 450°F (230°C) oven for 17 to 20 minutes, or until the edges are golden.

Pizza Mediterranean

Prepare dough according to above recipe and roll onto pan. To make one pizza, top with 1 cup (250 ml) fresh chopped tomatoes mixed with 2 tbsp. (30 ml) of olive oil, 2 tbsp (30 ml) of aromatic preserve (see recipe, p. 17). Add 1 cup (250 ml) of shredded mozzarella cheese, 1 cup (250 ml) of sliced squid, 1/2 cup (120 ml) of baby shrimp, 1/2 cup (120 ml) of scallops, 1/2 cup (120 ml) of baby clams. Bake in a pre-heated 450°F (230°C) oven for 17 to 20 minutes, or until the edges are golden.

Pasta

Literally translated, pasta means "dough" or "paste." Italians have been eating pasta since the 13th century, and once regarded it as a luxury food reserved for special occasions and feasts.

The original pastas were made from barley, rye or spelt flours, but when wheat was introduced to Italy it became the common choice. Pasta is made by combining water with durum semolina (hard wheat flour) and eggs are sometimes added for tenderness (pasta all'uovo). There is a wide selection of pasta shapes and sizes on the market today which you can buy dried or fresh. The cuts fall under one of two categories: *spaghetti* (long pasta) or *maccheroni* (short pasta).

Dried pasta (*pasta secca*) has a long shelf life and retains a firm texture when cooked. Fresh pasta (*pasta fresca*), if you can buy it or make it yourself, is made from soft wheat and is the preferred choice. It cooks more quickly, has a softer texture, and simply tastes better. You can also buy flavoured pastas like spinach, beet, saffron, or sun-dried tomato pasta.

I like to call pasta the food of fantasy because it allows a cook the freedom to use the imagination and create a truly unique dish. There are not many ingredients that do not go well with pasta.

Pasta is traditionally served as a *primo piatto* (first course) as is soup or risotto, but most of these pasta recipes can also be served as a main course.

Cooking Pasta

Pasta requires a lot of water to cook properly. A good rule of thumb is to use 4 quarts (4 litres) of water and 2 tablespoons (30 ml) of salt for every pound (450 g) of pasta. Always bring the salted water to a rolling boil first before slowly adding in your pasta. A tablespoon of oil added to the water will help prevent sticking, but make sure you stir your pasta occasionally. If your homemade fresh pasta froths too much while cooking, you probably left too much excess flour on the dough. Dust off your dough before cooking to minimize the frothing.

Cooking time depends on the pasta shape and size, and whether it is fresh, which will take a shorter time, or dried, which will take longer. The best way to check if it is done is to taste it. It should be tender but firm (*al dente*), and have no taste of flour. To check commercial pasta, take a strand or piece from the pot and break it in half. If there is no white core, it should be done. The commercial dried brands usually take between 8 to 10 minutes to cook, while fresh pasta cooks much more quickly and will rise to the surface of the water when done. Cuts like ravioli and tortellini will take longer to cook because they are stuffed.

When you drain your pasta, always retain a bit of the cooking water in case your pasta absorbs too much of the sauce you are serving it with and becomes dry. And please do not rinse off your pasta with cold water unless you are preparing *pasta al forno* (baked pasta) and need to handle it. Rinsing your pasta spoils the flavour and texture, and prevents your sauce from sticking.

Pasta all' Uovo
Fresh Egg Pasta

All-purpose flour	4 cups	1 litre
Durum semolina	1 cup	250 ml
Large eggs	4	4
Water	1 cup	250 ml
Vegetable or olive oil	2 tbsp.	30 ml
Salt	1 tbsp.	20 ml

Combine the flour with the durum semolina and mound it onto your work surface. Make a hollow in the middle so that it resembles a nest. Into this nest, break your eggs and add the oil, salt, and a bit of the water. Beat this mixture with a fork, and gradually begin to mix in the surrounding flour, adding more water as needed, until a thick pastry ball has formed. Continue mixing with your hands until the dough cannot incorporate any more flour and it does not stick to the work surface. If the dough is sticky, add more flour. If the dough will not stick together, add some more water. Making sure that your work surface is floured, knead the dough by pushing it with the heels of your hands.

Finishing By Hand

If you are not using a pasta machine, continue to knead for 5 to 10 minutes, until the dough is smooth and elastic. Divide the dough into four sections and roll each one out to about 1/8-inch (6-mm) thickness. Cut the dough into whatever pasta shapes you want.

Finishing Using Pasta Machine

If you have a pasta machine, the process is much easier and saves you the rolling-out process. First run your section of dough through the rollers at the widest setting. Fold the flattened dough over once and run it through again. Continue this process a few more times until the dough is smooth and elastic. To thin out the dough, set the machine to the next lowest number and run the pasta sheet through the rollers. Continue this process, lowering the roller setting each time until you achieve the desired thickness. You may have to cut your pasta sheet to make it workable, as it will get longer each time it passes through the machine. To cut the pasta, run the thin pasta sheet through the cutting rollers, which are set on the cut you prefer. Lasagna can be cut by hand, and the full width of the machine is about right for cannelloni.

Makes about 2 pounds (1 kilogram) of pasta.

Variation

Fresh coloured pasta is interesting and easy to make, once you learn the basics of making fresh pasta, as instructed above. Try mixing and matching different coloured pastas for an attractive display. Here is a guideline when making coloured pastas, using the above pasta recipe as a base.

Green pasta

Pasta verde uses spinach to achieve its lovely colour. To the above recipe add 12 ounces (340 g) of fresh spinach, which will take the place of the water. Cook the spinach for five minutes and then drain. Chop it as finely as possible, until it is like a paste. Follow the recipe instructions as directed.

Orange pasta

Into the pasta mixture, stir in 1 cup (250 ml) of tomato sauce or puréed tomatoes. Adjust the water amount as necessary.

Red pasta

In a food processor, purée 1 pound (454 g) of cooked or canned beets. Add to the pasta mixture and adjust the water amount as necessary.

Yellow pasta

Combine 1/8 teaspoon (1 ml) of saffron with the flour and mix well before incorporating the oil and eggs.

Pasta con Sugo di Carne
Pasta with Meat Sauce

Pasta, your choice	1 lb.	450 g
Olive oil	3 tbsp.	50 ml
Onion, chopped	1	1
Garlic clove, minced	1	1
Celery stalk, chopped	1	1
Carrot, peeled and chopped	1	1
Ground meat (beef, veal, and/or pork)	1 lb.	450 g
Strained tomatoes	1 cup	250 ml
Chicken broth (see recipe, p. 39)	3/4 cup	180 ml
Red wine	1/2 cup	120 ml
Basil	1 pinch	1 pinch
Nutmeg, grated	1 pinch	1 pinch
Chopped parsley, to taste		
Salt and pepper, to taste		
Parmesan cheese, grated	3 tbsp.	50 ml

Bring a large pot of salted water to a boil. Add pasta and boil according to package directions. In a saucepan, heat oil and sauté onion, garlic, celery, carrot, and meat until lightly browned. Add remaining ingredients, except cheese, and simmer for 15 minutes until thick, stirring occasionally. Drain pasta and toss with sauce and cheese.

Makes 4 to 6 servings.

Spaghetti con Salsa Rosata
Spaghetti with Rosé Sauce

The word spaghetti translates as "little strings."

Spaghetti	1 lb.	450 g
Olive oil	1/4 cup	60 ml
Onion, chopped	1	1
Garlic clove, minced	2	2
Strained tomatoes	1 cup	250 ml
35% cream	1/2 cup	120 ml
Red wine	1/2 cup	120 ml

Dried basil	1 tsp.	5 ml
Nutmeg, grated	1 pinch	1 pinch
Chopped parsley, to taste		
Salt and pepper, to taste		
Parmesan cheese, grated	3 tbsp.	50 ml

Bring a large pot of salted water to a boil. Add pasta and cook according to package directions. In a fry pan, heat oil and sauté onion and garlic until lightly browned. Add remaining ingredients except cheese and simmer for 12 to 15 minutes, stirring occasionally. Drain pasta and toss with sauce and cheese.

Makes 4 to 6 servings.

Spaghetti con Peperoni Verdi e Pomodoro
Spaghetti with Green Pepper and Tomato Sauce

Spaghetti	1 lb.	450 g
Olive oil	3 tbsp.	50 ml
Onion, chopped	1	1
Garlic clove, minced	1	1
Pancetta	4 oz.	115g
Green pepper, chopped	1	1
Chicken broth (see recipe, p. 39)	3/4 cup	180 ml
Strained or peeled tomatoes	1 cup	250 ml
Tomato paste	1 tbsp.	15 ml
(add only if using peeled tomatoes)		
White or Red wine	1/2 cup	120 ml
Dried basil	1 pinch	1 pinch
Chili pepper	1 pinch	1 pinch
Salt and pepper, to taste		
Parmesan or Romano cheese	3 tbsp.	50 ml
Parsley, chopped, to taste		

Bring a large pot of salted water to a boil. Add spaghetti and cook according to package directions. In a saucepan, heat oil and sauté onion, garlic, pancetta, and green pepper until lightly browned. Add remaining ingredients, except cheese and parsley, and simmer for 12 to 15 minutes over moderate heat, stirring occasionally. Drain pasta and toss with sauce, grated cheese and parsley.

Makes 4 to 6 servings.

Linguine alla Genovese
Genoa-Style Linguini

"Alla genovese" usually refers to a dish made with olive oil, garlic and herbs, particularly basil. Similar to a pesto.

Linguine	1 lb.	450 g
Olive oil	1/4 cup	60 ml
Butter	3 tbsp.	50 ml
Garlic cloves, minced	2	2
Fresh basil, chopped	1/2 cup	120 ml
Pine nuts or walnuts, chopped	1/2 cup	120 ml
Pecorino Romano cheese	3/4 cup	180 ml
Crushed peppercorn	1 tbsp.	15 ml
Salt, to taste		

Bring a pot of salted water to a boil. Add pasta and cook according to package directions. In a large skillet, heat oil and butter and sauté garlic for 1 minute. In a blender or food processor, combine heated oil and garlic with remaining ingredients and blend until smooth. Drain the pasta and toss with pesto sauce until well coated.

Makes 4 to 6 servings.

Paglia e Fieno
Fresh Pasta with Tomato, Chicken and Cream Sauce

This dish is literally translated as "straw and hay."

Fresh spinach noodles	1 lb.	450 g
Fresh egg noodles	1 lb.	450 g
Olive oil	1/4 cup	60 ml
Butter	2 tbsp.	30 ml
Green onions, chopped	2	2
Chicken breast, skinned, de-boned, and diced	1/2	1/2
Tomatoes, peeled and chopped	1 1/2 cup	375 ml
Chicken broth (see recipe, p. 39)	1/2 cup	120 ml
Chopped parsley, to taste		
Salt and pepper, to taste		

35% cream	1/2 cup	120 ml
Parmesan or Romano cheese	1/2 cup	120 ml

Bring a large pot of salted water to a boil. Add fresh pasta noodles and cook until tender, stirring occasionally. In a large skillet, heat oil and butter and sauté onions and chicken for 4 to 6 minutes. Add remaining ingredients except cream and cheese. Lower heat to medium and simmer for 10 to 14 minutes, stirring occasionally. Drain the pasta and toss with the sauce, cream and grated cheese until well coated.

Makes 4 to 6 servings.

Fettuccine Fresche alla Panna
Fresh Fettuccine with Cream Sauce

Fettuccine are long, flat ribbons of pasta. You may also use tagliatelle, which are similar. Also called Fettucine al Fredo.

Fresh fettuccine	2 lbs.	900 g
Chicken broth (see recipe, p. 39)	1 cup	250 ml
35% cream	2 cups	500 ml
White wine	1/2 cup	120 ml
Butter	1/4 cup	60 ml
Olive oil	1/4 cup	60 ml
Green onions, chopped	2	2
Nutmeg	1 pinch	1 pinch
Salt and pepper, to taste		
All-purpose flour	3 tbsp.	50 ml
Parmesan cheese, grated	1/2 cup	120 ml
Fresh parsley, chopped	2 tbsp.	30 ml

Bring a large pot of salted water to a boil. Add fettuccine and cook for about 10 minutes, stirring gently. In a second pot, combine broth, cream and wine and bring to a boil. In a fry pan, heat butter and oil and sauté the onion, nutmeg, salt and pepper until lightly browned. Stir in flour to make a roux. Stir in the cream mixture and bring back to a boil for a few minutes. Drain the pasta and toss with the sauce, cheese and parsley.

Makes 4 to 6 servings.

Capellini alla Pastorella
Capellini with Oyster Mushroom and Cream Sauce

Capellini, which means "little hairs," are very thin strands of spaghetti. Taleggio is a soft, mild cow's milk cheese. You could substitute Bel Paese or Mozzarella.

Capellini	1 lb.	450 g
Olive oil	3 tbsp.	50 ml
Shallots, chopped	2	2
Oyster mushrooms, sliced	1 cup	250 ml
Red pepper, chopped	1/2	1/2
Chicken broth	1/2 cup	120 ml
(see recipe, p. 39)		
35% cream	3/4 cup	180 ml
Chopped parsley, to taste		
Salt and pepper, to taste		
Taleggio cheese, grated	3/4 cup	180 ml

Bring a large pot of salted water to a boil. Add capellini and cook according to package directions. In a large skillet, heat oil and sauté shallots, mushrooms and red pepper until lightly browned. Lower heat to medium and stir in remaining ingredients except cheese. Simmer for 5 to 7 minutes, stirring occasionally. Drain the pasta and toss with sauce and cheese.

Makes 4 to 6 servings.

Tortellini al Pomodoro
Tortellini with Tomato Sauce

Tortellini means "little cakes." You can substitute ravioli if you like.

Tortellini	2 lbs.	900 g
Olive oil	3 tbsp.	50 ml
Onion, chopped	1/2	1/2
Garlic clove, minced	1	1
Strained tomatoes	1 cup	250 ml
Chicken broth	1/2 cup	120 ml
(see recipe, p. 39)		

Red or White wine	1/2 cup	120 ml
Dried basil	1/2 tsp.	2 ml
Chopped parsley, to taste		
Salt and pepper, to taste		
Parmesan cheese, grated	1/4 cup	60 ml

Bring a large pot of salted water to a boil. Add tortellini and cook for 12 to 15 minutes, or until tender. In a saucepan, heat oil and sauté onion and garlic for 2 minutes. Add remaining ingredients, except cheese, and simmer over moderate heat for 10 to 15 minutes, stirring occasionally. Drain the tortellini and toss with the sauce and cheese. Sprinkle with chili pepper, if desired.

Makes 4 servings.

Tortellini con Salsa di Funghi e Crema
Tortellini with Mushroom Sauce

Tortellini	2 lbs.	900 g
Olive oil	1/4 cup	60 ml
Onion, chopped	1/2	1/2
Garlic clove, minced	1	1
Large mushrooms, sliced	6	6
Chicken broth (see recipe, p. 39)	3/4 cup	180 ml
35% cream (optional)	1/2 cup	120 ml
White or Red wine	1/2 cup	120 ml
Strained or peeled tomatoes	1 cup	250 ml
Basil	1 pinch	1 pinch
Nutmeg	1 pinch	1 pinch
Salt and pepper, to taste		
Chopped parsley, to taste		
Parmesan or Romano cheese	1/4 cup	60 ml

Bring a large pot of salted water to a boil. Add tortellini and cook for 15 to 20 minutes, or until tender. In a large fry pan, heat the oil and sauté the onion, garlic and mushrooms for 4 to 5 minutes. Add remaining ingredients, except cheese and simmer for 12 to 15 minutes over moderate heat, stirring occasionally. Drain the tortellini and toss with sauce and cheese.

Makes 4 servings.

Linguine con Salmone Affumicato
Linguini with Smoked Salmon Sauce

Linguine, which means "little tongues," are narrow, flat ribbons of pasta, thinner than fettuccine.

Linguine	1 lb.	450 g
Butter	2 tbsp.	30 ml
Oil	2 tbsp.	30 ml
Green onions, chopped	4	4
Green pepper, sliced thin	1/2	1/2
Chicken broth (see recipe, p. 39)	1/2 cup	120 ml
White wine	1/2 cup	120 ml
Tomatoes, peeled or strained	1 cup	250 ml
35% cream	1/2 cup	120 ml
Smoked salmon, chopped	1/2 cup	120 ml
Chopped parsley, to taste		
Salt and pepper, to taste		
Parmesan cheese (optional)	2 tbsp.	30 ml

Bring a large pot of salted water to a boil. Add linguine and cook according to package directions. In a large saucepan, heat butter and oil and sauté onions and pepper for 2 to 3 minutes. Add the broth, wine, and tomatoes and simmer over moderate heat for 8 to 10 minutes, stirring occasionally. Add the cream, salmon, parsley, salt and pepper and cook for an additional 2 minutes. Drain the pasta and toss with the sauce and some grated cheese, if preferred.

Makes 4 to 6 servings.

Spaghettini con Peperoni Verdi e Tonno
Spaghettini with Green Pepper and Tuna Fish Sauce

Spaghettini are just a thinner version of spaghetti, similar to capelli d'angelo.

Spaghettini	1 lb.	450 g
Olive oil	3 tbsp.	50 ml
Onion, chopped	1	1
Garlic clove, minced	1	1
Green pepper, diced	1	1
Chicken broth (see recipe, p. 39)	3/4 cup	180 ml
White wine	1/2 cup	120 ml
Tomatoes, strained or peeled	1 cup	250 ml

Dried basil	1 pinch	1 pinch
Dried sage	1 pinch	1 pinch
Chili pepper	1 pinch	1 pinch
Chopped parsley, to taste		
Salt and pepper, to taste		
Canned tuna, drained	7 oz.	200 g
Parmesan or Romano cheese	3 tbsp.	50 ml

Bring a large pot of salted water to a boil. Add spaghettini and cook according to package directions. In a large fry pan, heat the oil and sauté the onion, garlic, and green pepper for 2 to 3 minutes. Add the remaining ingredients, except the tuna and cheese. Simmer for 10 to 14 minutes, stirring occasionally. Drain the pasta. Toss with the sauce, tuna and grated cheese until well coated.

Makes 4 to 6 servings.

Linguine con Vongole
Linguini with White Clam Sauce

Linguine	1 lb.	450 g
Olive oil	2 tbsp.	30 ml
Butter	2 tbsp.	30 ml
Onion, chopped	1	1
Green onions, chopped	2	2
Garlic clove, minced	1	1
Chicken broth (see recipe, p. 39)	1/2 cup	120 ml
White wine	1/4 cup	60 ml
35% cream	1/2 cup	120 ml
Pernod or Maraschino juice	2 tbsp.	30 ml
Brandy	2 tbsp.	30 ml
Tin of baby clams, drained (or 2 lbs./1 kg fresh baby clams)	10 oz.	285 ml
Dried sage	1 pinch	1 pinch
Chili pepper	1 pinch	1 pinch
Chopped parsley, to taste		
Salt and pepper, to taste		

Bring a large pot of salted water to a boil. Add linguine and cook according to package directions. In a large fry pan, heat oil and butter and sauté onion, green onions, and garlic until slightly browned. Add remaining ingredients and simmer over moderate heat for 10 minutes. Drain pasta and add to fry pan. Toss with sauce until well coated.

Makes 4 to 6 servings.

Spaghetti con Cozze e Pomodoro
Spaghetti with Mussels and Tomato Sauce

Spaghetti	1 lb.	450 g
Oil	1/4 cup	60 ml
Butter	2 tbsp.	30 ml
Onion, chopped	1	1
Garlic cloves, minced	2	2
Tomatoes, peeled and chopped	1 cup	250 ml
Tomato paste	1 tbsp.	15 ml
Chicken broth (see recipe, p. 39)	3/4 cup	180 ml
White wine	1/2 cup	120 ml
Dried sage	1 pinch	1 pinch
Chili pepper	1 pinch	1 pinch
Salt and pepper, to taste		
Fresh mussels, scrubbed and de-bearded OR 1 tin of mussels in brine	2 dozen	2 dozen
Fresh parsley, chopped	1 tbsp.	15 ml
Parmesan or Romano cheese	2 tbsp.	30 ml

Bring a large pot of salted water to a boil. Add the spaghetti and cook according to package directions. Place the mussels in a pot with some water. Cover and steam until open. In a saucepan, heat the oil and butter and sauté the onion and garlic until translucent. Add tomatoes, tomato paste, broth, wine, sage, chili pepper, salt and pepper. Simmer for 10 minutes over moderate heat, stirring occasionally. Add mussels and simmer for an additional 5 minutes. Drain the pasta and toss with the sauce, parsley and grated cheese.

Makes 4 to 6 servings.

Spaghettini con Aragosta
Spaghettini with Lobster Sauce

Spaghetti	1 lb.	450 g
Olive oil	3 tbsp.	50 ml
Butter	2 tbsp.	30 ml
Onion, chopped (or 4 shallots, chopped)	1/2	1/2
Garlic clove, minced	1	1
Red or green pepper, diced	1/2	1/2
Tomatoes, peeled or strained	1 cup	250 ml

White wine	1/2 cup	120 ml
35% cream or boiling milk	1/2 cup	120 ml
Canned lobster meat, diced	11 oz.	310 g
Chili pepper	1 pinch	1 pinch
Salt and pepper, to taste		
Chopped parsley, to taste		
Parmesan or Romano cheese	3 tbsp.	50 ml

Bring a large pot of salted water to a boil. Add spaghetti and cook according to package directions. In a large fry pan, heat the oil and butter and sauté the onion, garlic, and pepper for 2 to 3 minutes, until lightly browned. Add the remaining ingredients, except the parsley and cheese. Simmer over moderate heat for 12 to 14 minutes, stirring occasionally. Drain the pasta and toss with the sauce, parsley and grated cheese.

Makes 4 to 6 servings.

Fettuccine Verdi con Ventagli Pettino e Salsa Rosata
Spinach Fettuccine with Scallops and Rosé Sauce

Spinach fettuccine	1 lb.	450 g
Olive oil	3 tbsp.	50 ml
Onion, chopped	1	1
Garlic clove, minced	1	1
Chicken broth (see recipe, p. 39)	3/4 cup	180 ml
White wine (optional)	1/2 cup	120 ml
Tomatoes, peeled or strained	1 cup	250 ml
Dried sage	1 tsp.	5 ml
Chili pepper	1 pinch	1 pinch
Salt and pepper, to taste		
Medium scallops	2 cups	500 ml
10% cream or boiling milk	1/2 cup	120 ml
Parmesan cheese, grated	1/4 cup	60 ml
Chopped parsley, for garnish		

Bring a large pot of salted water to a boil. Add fettuccine and cook according to package directions. In a saucepan, heat oil and sauté onion and garlic until lightly browned. Add remaining ingredients, except scallops, cream, cheese, and parsley. Simmer for 10 to 12 minutes, stirring occasionally. Drain the pasta and toss with sauce, scallops, cream and cheese until well incorporated. Sprinkle with parsley and serve.

Makes 4 to 6 servings.

Spaghetti con Gamberi e Capperi
Spaghetti with Shrimps and Caper Sauce

Spaghetti	1 lb.	450 g
Olive or vegetable oil	3 tbsp.	50 ml
Onion, chopped	1/2	1/2
Garlic clove, minced	1	1
Chicken broth (see recipe, p. 39)	1/2 cup	120 ml
White wine	1/2 cup	120 ml
Tomatoes, peeled	1 cup	250 ml
Small shrimps, peeled and de-veined	2 cups	500 ml
Capers	2 tbsp.	30 ml
Dried basil	1 pinch	1 pinch
Chili pepper	1 pinch	1 pinch
Salt and pepper, to taste		
Fresh parsley, chopped	2 tbsp.	30 ml
Romano or Parmesan cheese	2 tbsp.	30 ml

Bring a large pot of salted water to a boil. Add the spaghetti and cook according to package directions. In a saucepan, heat the oil and sauté the onion and garlic until lightly browned. Add remaining ingredients, except parsley and cheese. Simmer for 10 minutes over moderate heat, stirring occasionally. Drain the pasta and toss with sauce, parsley and cheese until well coated.

Makes 4 to 6 servings.

Pasta Fresca alla Mediterranea
Fresh Pasta with Mediterranean Seafood Sauce

Fresh pasta	2 lbs.	900 g
Olive oil	5 tbsp.	75 ml
Onion, finely chopped	1/2	1/2
Garlic cloves, minced	2	2
Calamari, cleaned and diced	2 cups	500 ml
Mussels, washed	10	10
Small clams, washed	10	10
Shrimp, peeled and de-veined	2 cups	500 ml
Tomatoes, peeled	1 cup	250 ml
White wine	1/2 cup	120 ml
Olives, chopped	1/2 cup	120 ml
Dried basil	1 tsp.	5 ml

Chili pepper, chopped	1 tsp.	5 ml
Chopped parsley, to taste		
Salt and pepper, to taste		

Bring a large pot of salted water to a boil. Add fresh pasta and cook until tender. In a large fry pan, heat oil and cook onion, garlic, calamari, mussels, and clams for 5 minutes, covered. Add remaining ingredients, except shrimp; lower heat to medium and simmer for 12 to 15 minutes, stirring occasionally. Add shrimp and cook 3 minutes longer. Drain pasta and transfer to a large serving dish. Top with the seafood sauce and serve.

Makes 4 to 6 servings.

Rigatoni alla Pescatore
Rigatoni with Seafood Sauce

"Alla pescatore" means "fisherman's style" and refers to any dish prepared with seafood.

Rigatoni	1 lb.	450 g
Olive oil	1/4 cup	60 ml
Onion, finely chopped	1	1
Garlic clove, minced	1	1
Squid, cleaned and chopped	8 oz.	225 g
Tomatoes, peeled	2 cups	500 ml
(or Tomato sauce, see recipe p. 27)		
Scallops	8 oz.	225 g
Shrimp, peeled and de-veined	8 oz.	225 g
Mussels, washed	1 lb.	450 g
White wine	1/2 cup	120 ml
Parsley, chopped	1/2 cup	120 ml
Chili pepper preserve (see recipe, p. 18)	1 tbsp.	15 ml
Salt and pepper, to taste		

Bring a large pot of salted water to a boil. Add rigatoni and cook according to package directions. In a large skillet, heat oil and sauté onion, garlic and squid for 5 minutes, stirring occasionally. Add tomatoes and simmer for 8 minutes over moderate heat. Add remaining ingredients and continue to simmer, stirring frequently. Drain pasta and toss with sauce until well coated.

Makes 4 to 6 servings.

Ravioli con Vegetali e Crema
Ravioli with Vegetables and Cream Sauce

Ravioli, which perhaps means "little turnips," is a square, stuffed pasta shape somewhat similar to tortellini.

Ravioli	2 lbs.	900 g
Olive oil	1/4 cup	60 ml
Onion, chopped	1/2	1/2
Garlic clove, minced	1	1
Carrot, shredded	1/2	1/2
Broccoli, diced	1 cup	250 ml
Mushrooms, sliced	6	6
Chicken broth (see recipe, p. 39)	1/2 cup	120 ml
White wine (optional)	1/2 cup	120 ml
35% cream	3/4 cup	180 ml
Tomato, chopped	1	1
Green pepper, diced	1/2	1/2
Salt and pepper, to taste		
Chopped parsley, to taste		
Romano cheese, grated	1/4 cup	60 ml

Bring a large pot of salted water to a boil. Add ravioli and cook until tender. In a large fry pan, heat oil and sauté onion, garlic, carrots, broccoli and mushrooms 6 to 8 minutes, or until tender. Add remaining ingredients, except parsley and cheese and simmer for 6 more minutes, stirring occasionally. Drain the ravioli and toss with the sauce, parsley and cheese.

Makes 4 to 6 servings.

Perciatelli con Carciofi e Pomodoro
Perciatelli with Artichoke and Tomato Sauce

Perciatelli are similar to long, hollow strands of spaghetti.

Perciatelli	1 lb.	450 g
Olive oil	1/4 cup	60 ml
Onion, chopped	1/2	1/2
Garlic clove, minced	1	1

Pancetta, chopped	4 oz.	115 g
Artichoke hearts, drained and sliced	6 oz. jar	170 ml
Chicken broth (see recipe, p. 39)	3/4 cup	180 ml
Red wine	1/2 cup	120 ml
Tomatoes, strained	1 cup	250 ml
Dried basil	1 pinch	1 pinch
Salt and pepper, to taste		
Parmesan cheese, grated	1/4 cup	60 ml

Bring a large pot of salted water to a boil. Add the pasta and cook according to package directions. In a large fry pan, heat oil and sauté onion, garlic, and pancetta until lightly browned. Add remaining ingredients, except cheese. Simmer for 12 to 14 minutes, stirring occasionally. Drain the pasta and toss with the sauce and cheese.

Makes 4 to 6 servings.

Conchiglie con Olive e Carciofi
Jumbo Shells with Olives and Artichokes

Jumbo shells, or short pasta	1 lb.	450 g
Olive oil	3 tbsp.	50 ml
Onion, chopped	1	1
Garlic clove, minced	1	1
Chicken broth (see recipe, p. 39)	1/2 cup	120 ml
Red or White wine (optional)	1/2 cup	120 ml
Tomatoes, peeled	1 cup	250 ml
Artichoke hearts, drained and sliced	6 oz. jar	170 ml
Stuffed olives, sliced	1/2 cup	120 ml
Nutmeg	1 pinch	1 pinch
Salt and pepper, to taste		
Parmesan or Romano cheese	3 tbsp.	50 ml
Chopped parsley, to taste		

Bring a large pot of salted water to a boil. Add pasta and cook according to   package directions. In a fry pan, heat oil and sauté onion and garlic until lightly browned. Add broth, wine and tomatoes and simmer for 6 to 8 minutes, stirring occasionally. Add remaining ingredients, except cheese and parsley. Continue to simmer for 5 to 7 minutes. Drain the pasta and toss with the sauce, cheese and parsley.

Makes 4 to 6 servings.

Rotini con Pancetta e Pomodoro
Rotini with Pancetta and Tomato Sauce

Rotini is a short pasta shaped like a corkscrew, similar to fusilli but larger.

Rotini, or other short pasta	1 lb.	450 g
Olive oil	2 tbsp.	30 ml
Onion, chopped	1/2	1/2
Garlic clove, minced	1	1
Pancetta, sliced and diced	4 oz.	115 g
Chicken broth (see recipe, p. 39)	1/2 cup	120 ml
Red or White wine (optional)	1/2 cup	120 ml
Tomatoes, peeled or strained	1 cup	250 ml
Wine vinegar	1 tbsp.	15 ml
Dried basil	1 pinch	1 pinch
Chili pepper	1 pinch	1 pinch
Salt and pepper, to taste		
Chopped parsley, to taste		
Parmesan or Romano cheese	3 tbsp.	50 ml

Bring a large pot of salted water to a boil. Add rotini and cook according to package directions. In a large fry pan, heat oil and sauté onion, garlic, and pancetta until lightly browned. Add remaining ingredients, except parsley and cheese. Simmer for 12 to 15 minutes, stirring occasionally. Drain the pasta and toss with the sauce and cheese. Sprinkle with parsley before serving.

Makes 4 to 6 servings.

Spaghetti di Spinaci con Prosciutto Cotto e Cognac
Spinach Spaghetti with Cooked Ham and Cognac

Spinach spaghetti	1 lb.	450 g
Olive oil	1/4 cup	60 ml
Green onions, chopped	4	4
Garlic clove, minced	1	1
Italian cooked ham, diced	4 oz.	115 g
Chicken broth (see recipe, p. 39)	3/4 cup	180 ml
Strained tomatoes	1 1/2 cups	375 ml
Cognac	1/2 cup	120 ml
Chili pepper	1 pinch	1 pinch

Italian cheeses and cured meats.
From the left to right: Auricchio and
Caciocavallo cheeses, Capicollo, two
long Salami, two Prociutti, Pancetta,
Soprassate, and a large round of
Asiago below.

Tomato sauce (page 27) is a basic ingredient in many Italian recipes.

Seafood Platter (page 33) is an antipasto that can be shared by everyone at the table.

Prosciutto and Melon, pictured here, or with fresh figs as in recipe on page 36.

Minestrone is a soup that can accommodate many ingredients. Here it is shown with beef (page 45).

Salt and pepper, to taste		
35% cream	1/2 cup	120 ml
Parmesan or Romano cheese	1/4 cup	60 ml
Chopped parsley, to taste		

Bring a large pot of salted water to a boil. Add spaghetti and cook according to package directions. In a saucepan, heat oil and sauté onions, garlic and ham for 2 to 3 minutes. Add remaining ingredients, except cream, cheese, and parsley. Simmer for 10 to 12 minutes over moderate heat, stirring occasionally. Drain the pasta and toss with the sauce, cream, cheese and parsley until well coated.

Makes 4 to 6 servings.

Spaghetti Amatriciana
Spaghetti with Pancetta and Chili Pepper Sauce

All' Amatriciana *refers to a town on the border of Latium and Abruzzo and means "Amatrice style." This pasta sauce is usually made with pancetta, onion, chili pepper, tomato and cheese.*

Spaghetti	1 lb.	450 g
Olive oil	3 tbsp.	50 ml
Onion, chopped	1/2	1/2
Garlic clove, minced	1	1
Pancetta, chopped	1 cup	250 ml
Chicken broth (see recipe, p. 39)	1/2 cup	120 ml
Red wine	1/2 cup	120 ml
Tomatoes, peeled	1 1/4 cups	300 ml
Tomato paste	2 tbsp.	30 ml
Red wine vinegar	2 tbsp.	30 ml
Chili pepper	2 tsp.	10 ml
Salt and pepper, to taste		
Parmesan cheese, grated	1/2 cup	120 ml

Bring a large pot of salted water to a boil. Add spaghetti and cook according to package directions. In a large skillet, heat oil and sauté onion, garlic, and pancetta for 2 to 3 minutes. Add remaining ingredients, except cheese, and mix well. Lower heat to medium and simmer for 12 to 15 minutes, stirring occasionally. Drain the pasta and toss with the sauce and cheese.

Makes 4 to 6 servings.

Pappardelle con Salsa di Funghi, Prosciutto e Crema
Pappardelle with Mushroom, Prosciutto and Cream Sauce

Pappardelle is a long, flat cut of pasta, 1 inch wide by 6 inches (2.5 x 15 cm) long, usually made with eggs.

Pappardelle	1 lb.	450 g
Vegetable oil	1/2 cup	120 ml
Onion, chopped	1	1
Prosciutto, chopped	1 cup	250 ml
Mushrooms, sliced	2 cups	500 ml
Chicken broth	1/2 cup	120 ml
(see recipe, p. 39)		
White wine	1/4 cup	60 ml
35% cream or boiling milk	1 cup	250 ml
Juice of 1/2 a lemon		
Dried basil	1 tbsp.	15 ml
Salt and pepper, to taste		
Parmesan cheese, grated	1 cup	250 ml
Parsley, chopped	1/2 cup	120 ml

Bring a large pot of salted water to a boil. Add pasta and cook according to package directions. In a large fry pan, heat oil and sauté onion, prosciutto and mushrooms for 3 minutes, stirring frequently. Lower the heat to medium and add remaining ingredients, except cheese and parsley. Simmer for 10 to 12 minutes, stirring occasionally. Drain the pasta and toss with the sauce, cheese and pasta.

Makes 4 servings.

Penne alla Rustica
Penne with Mushrooms and Green Pepper

Olive oil	1/4 cup	60 ml
Small onion, sliced	1	1
Garlic clove, chopped	1	1
Mushrooms, sliced	10	10
Green pepper, sliced	1	1
Salt and pepper, to taste		

Tomato sauce (see recipe, p. 27)	1 cup	250 ml
Peas	1/2 cup	120 ml
Black olives, pitted	1/2 cup	120 ml
Penne, cooked and drained	8 oz.	225 g
Parmesan cheese, grated	2 tbsp.	30 ml

Heat the oil in a fry pan and sauté the onion, garlic, mushrooms and green pepper for 5 minutes. Season with salt and pepper. Add the tomato sauce, peas, black olives and simmer for 15 minutes. Place the cooked penne on a serving platter. Pour the sauce on top and around the pasta. Sprinkle with the cheese and serve.

Serves 4.

Fish and Shellfish

The long stretches of Italian coastline on the Mediterranean, Adriatic and Tyrrhenian seas provide a vast selection of fish (*pesce*) and shellfish (*crostacei*) for use in Italian cooking. Perhaps that is why fish is such a popular and important part of an Italian meal.

It may be a good idea to add some more fish to your diet. It contains a lot of protein, minerals, and vitamins, but very little fat. And, of course, it tastes great.

Fish is sometimes served as a separate course, but is normally a main course dish or *piatto di mezzo*.

Buying Fish

When buying fresh fish, use your eyes, your nose, and your fingers. First, look at the fish. Its eyes should gleam, the scales should be tight to the flesh, and the gills should be red. Next, smell the fish. It should never have a strong, fishy odour. And third, touch the fish. Press the flesh between your finger and thumb. It should be firm and spring back when you let it go, and the scales should not leave a sticky film on your fingers. So, if a fresh fish has cloudy eyes, a fishy smell or sticky scales, don't buy it because it is too old.

If you are buying frozen fish, be sure it is completely hard with no ice on the outside of the package. Never thaw and re-freeze fish. Bring it straight home and put it in the freezer immediately. When it is time to defrost it, do it slowly in the refrigerator, or else it will lose flavour and become mushy.

Preparing and Cooking Fish

Fresh or well-frozen and properly thawed fish should have no odour, but if there is a fishy smell, you should wash the fish with salt and water and rinse it thoroughly. Combine oil, lemon juice, a pinch or oregano and curry powder. Marinate the fish in this mixture or cook the fish right in it.

If your cutting board or work area smells fishy, never wash it off with soap and water. The soap will trap the smell and make it worse. Instead, wash the surface with lemon juice and cold water.

Fresh or frozen fish can be poached, baked, cooked in foil, sautéed, or deep-fried. To test whether a fish is properly cooked, insert a knife under the flesh at the backbone. If the flesh lifts away easily, the fish is properly cooked and ready to fillet.

To fillet a cooked fish, first take a sharp knife and loosen the skin at the tail. Pull off the skin from the entire side of the fish. Cut off the head and tail. Run a knife along one side of the backbone, underneath the flesh and wiggle your knife gently until the fillet comes off in one piece. Repeat on the other side of the backbone.

To fillet a raw fish, lay the fish on its side and slice it behind the head and down the length of the backbone. Remove the fillet by placing the knife flat along the backbone and cutting downward, scraping away from the bones until the fillet comes away in one piece.

Crustaceans

This family of shellfish includes crab, lobster, crayfish, scampi, prawns and shrimp. If you are serving shellfish as your main course, always try to buy fresh, but if you only need a small amount for part of a recipe, frozen or canned will do.

Buying Lobster

Lobster meat can be bought frozen or in cans, but it can also be bought live and cooked fresh. If you are buying fresh, make sure the pincers are taped so that you don't have any mishaps. Some people prefer the female lobster and others the male. Turn the lobster over. If it is female, you will be able to see the pink eggs showing through; if male, two blue lines will be visible. for instructions on how to cook and prepare your lobster, refer to the individual recipes.

Buying and De-veining Shrimp

Shrimp are available canned or frozen, but fresh is best for cooking. If you buy them still in the shells, look for ones that fit snugly in their shells, are firm and don't smell fishy. Shrimp that have been frozen and then thawed look shrunken, and are limp and dull.

Shrimp can be peeled and de-veined before or after cooking. To remove the shell, split it between the legs and it will come off easily. To de-vein, scrape open the flesh on the top until you see a black line. Simply scrape this away with a knife or toothpick.

Mollusks

Mollusks are soft, invertebrate animals enclosed in a hard, hinged shell.

They include clams, oysters, mussels, scallops and snails. If you are buying fresh, avoid ones whose shells are even slightly open, as they are close to dying. A fresh mollusk will have a tightly closed shell and no smell. To loosen the sand from the crevices in the shell, soak the mollusks for 30 minutes in salt water before washing. Then scrub with a hard bristled brush and rinse thoroughly.

To open a raw oyster, first protect the hand holding the oyster by wrapping it with a towel. Insert the tip of an oyster knife in the hinge of the shell and turn the knife until the shell opens. Run the knife around the top of the oyster to loosen it from the shell. To enjoy a raw oyster, don't chew it. It is better to swallow it whole.

Another class of mollusks is the cephalopods, which include squid, cuttlefish and octopus. Buy them fresh and make sure they smell like seawater and have firm flesh that does not leave a sticky film on your fingers.

Filetti di Merluzzo con Porri, e Pomodoro
Cod Fillets with Leeks and Tomatoes

Cod fillets	2 lbs.	900 g
All-purpose flour	2 tbsp.	30 ml
Vegetable oil	1/2 cup	120 ml
Sauce:		
Butter	3 tbsp.	50 ml
Leek, julienned	1	1
Garlic cloves, minced	2	2
Tomatoes, strained	1 cup	250 ml
White wine	1/2 cup	120 ml
Lemon juice	1/4 cup	60 ml
Aromatic preserve (see recipe, p. 17)	2 tbsp.	30 ml
Salt and pepper, to taste		

To make the sauce, heat butter in a fry pan and sauté leeks and garlic for 2 minutes, stirring occasionally. Add remaining ingredients and simmer over moderate heat for 8 minutes. In another fry pan, heat oil. Coat the fillets in flour and sauté them in the oil for 3 minutes on each side. Add in sauce, lower the heat to medium and simmer an additional few minutes.

Makes 4 servings.

Filetti di Limanda con Pinoli
Flounder Fillets with Pine Nut Sauce

8 Flounder fillets	4–5 oz. each	115–140g each
Flour	3 tbsp.	50 ml
Olive oil	1/4 cup	60 ml

Sauce:

Butter	2 tbsp.	30 ml
Green onions, chopped	2	2
Pine nuts	1/2 cup	120 ml
Flour	1 tbsp.	15 ml
Fish or chicken broth	1/2 cup	120 ml
(see recipes, p. 41/39)		
White wine	1/2 cup	120 ml
35% cream	1/2 cup	120 ml
Juice of 1 lemon		
Salt and pepper, to taste		
Parsley, chopped (for garnish)	1 tbsp.	15 ml

To make the sauce, heat the butter in a large fry pan and sauté onions until lightly browned. Add the pine nuts and cook for 2 minutes. Stir in flour, mixing well. Add remaining ingredients, except parsley, and simmer for 10 to 12 minutes, stirring occasionally. In another fry pan, heat the oil. Dust the fillets with flour and sauté for 3 to 4 minutes on each side. Add the sauce and bring to a boil. Sprinkle with parsley and serve.

Makes 8 servings.

Trance d'Ippoglosso con Cipolline e Funghi
Halibut Steaks with Shallots and Mushrooms

4 Halibut steaks	8 oz. each	225 g each
Vegetable oil	1/4 cup	60 ml
Mixed fresh herbs, chopped	3 tbsp.	50 ml
Mushrooms, sliced	2 cups	500 ml
Shallots, chopped	1 cup	250 ml
Fish or chicken broth	1/2 cup	120 ml
(see recipes, p. 41/39)		

White wine	1/2 cup	120 ml
Lemon juice	1/2 cup	120 ml
Salt and pepper, to taste		

Marinate the steaks in the oil and fresh herbs for about 10 minutes. Place the steaks in a heated fry pan and cover. Cook over medium heat for 3 minutes on each side. Add the remaining ingredients and simmer, covered, for another 6 minutes until done.

Makes 4 to 6 servings.

Triglie al Brandy
Red Mullet with Brandy

Red mullet is a bony saltwater fish with an edible liver.

Mullets, cleaned and scaled	2 lbs.	900 g
Flour	2 tbsp.	30 ml
Olive oil	5 tbsp.	75 ml
Sauce:		
Butter	3 tbsp.	50 ml
Green onions, chopped	4	4
Fish or chicken broth	1/2 cup	120 ml
(see recipes, p. 41/39)		
Brandy	1/2 cup	120 ml
Juice of 1/2 a lemon		
Fresh parsley, chopped	1/4 cup	60 ml
Sage	1 pinch	1 pinch
Salt and pepper, to taste		

To make sauce, heat butter and sauté green onions in a fry pan until translucent. Add remaining ingredients and simmer over moderate heat for 8 minutes. In another fry pan, heat oil and cook mullets for 5 minutes on each side. Add the sauce and simmer over moderate heat, covered, until fish is tender.

Tip: When the flesh comes easily away from the bone, the fish is done.

Makes 4 servings.

Filetto di Persico con Capperi e Wino
Fillet of Perch with Wine and Capers

Perch fillets	1 lb.	450 g
Olive oil	1/4 cup	60 ml
Sauce:		
Butter	3 tbsp.	50 ml
Onion, chopped	1	1
Garlic clove, minced	1	1
Chicken broth (see recipe, p. 39)	1/2 cup	120 ml
White wine	1/2 cup	120 ml
Tomatoes, strained or peeled	1 cup	250 ml
Capers	2 tbsp.	30 ml
Juice of 1/2 a lemon		
Chopped parsley, to taste		
Salt and pepper, to taste		

To make the sauce, heat the butter in a saucepan and sauté the onion and garlic until lightly browned. Add remaining ingredients and simmer over moderate heat for 10 to 14 minutes, stirring frequently. In another fry pan, heat oil and cook perch fillets, covered, until tender. Add the sauce and simmer for an additional few minutes.

Makes 4 servings.

Sandra con Cipollina e Vino Bianco
Pickerel with Shallots and Wine Sauce

Medium pickerels, cleaned	2	2
Flour	3 tbsp.	50 ml
Olive oil	1/4 cup	60 ml
Sauce:		
Butter	3 tbsp.	50 ml
Shallots, sliced	6	6
Garlic clove, minced	1	1
Red pepper, diced	1/2	1/2
Fish or chicken broth	1/2 cup	120 ml
(see recipes, p. 41/39)		

White wine	1/2 cup	120 ml
Lemon juice	1/3 cup	90 ml
Fennel seeds, crushed	1 tsp.	5 ml
Fresh parsley, chopped	1/2 cup	120 ml
Salt and pepper, to taste		

To make the sauce, heat butter in a fry pan. Sauté shallots, garlic and pepper until lightly browned. Add remaining ingredients and simmer 6 to 8 minutes, stirring occasionally. In another fry pan, heat oil. Dust pickerels with flour and place in fry pan. Cook, covered, for 6 to 8 minutes on each side. Add the sauce and continue to cook until fish is tender.

Makes 4 servings.

Trance di Salmone Giardiniera
Garden-Style Braised Salmon Steak

Olive oil	1/4 cup	60 ml
Leeks or green onions, chopped	1/2 cup	120 ml
Red pepper, diced	1 cup	250 ml
4 Salmon steaks	8 oz. each	225g each
Fish or chicken broth	1 cup	250 ml
(see recipes, p. 41/39)		
White wine	1/2 cup	120 ml
Lemon juice	1/2 cup	120 ml
Tomatoes, chopped	1/2 cup	120 ml
Dried thyme	1 tsp.	5 ml
Salt and pepper, to taste		

In a large fry pan, heat oil and sauté leeks and pepper for 3 minutes, stirring occasionally. Add salmon steaks and remaining ingredients. Lower heat to medium and cook, covered, for 8 to 10 minutes.

Tip: To check if the fish is done, insert a fork into the bone and if the bone comes out easily, the fish is cooked.

Transfer fish to a serving platter and top with the sauce.

Makes 4 servings.

Filetto di Salmone con Senape e Vino
Fillet of Salmon with Mustard and Wine Sauce

4 Salmon fillets	6–8 oz. each	170–225g each
Marinade:		
Olive oil	1/4 cup	60 ml
Dry mustard	1 tbsp.	15 ml
Crushed peppercorn	1 tsp.	5 ml
Sauce:		
Butter	2 tbsp.	30 ml
Olive oil	1 tbsp.	15 ml
Green onions, chopped	4	4
All-purpose flour	1 tbsp.	15 ml
Fish or chicken broth	1/2 cup	120 ml
(see recipes, p. 41/39)		
White wine	1/2 cup	120 ml
35% cream or boiled milk	1/2 cup	120 ml
Juice of 1 lemon		
Salt and pepper, to taste		
Chopped parsley, to taste (for garnish)		

Combine all ingredients for the marinade. Add salmon fillets and marinate for 15 to 30 minutes. In a large fry pan, heat the butter and oil. Sauté the green onion until lightly browned. Stir in flour, mixing well. Add remaining ingredients and allow mixture to reduce for 8 to 10 minutes, stirring occasionally. Heat another fry pan and cook marinated fillets, covered, for 3 to 4 minutes on each side. Add the sauce and simmer an additional few minutes. Sprinkle with parsley and serve.

Makes 4 servings.

Scorfano al Vino Bianco e Pomodoro
Red Snapper with White Wine and Tomato Sauce

4 Red snappers, cleaned	10–12 oz. each	285–340g each
Marinade:		
Olive oil	1/4 cup	60 ml
Dried sage	1 tsp.	5 ml

Dried basil	1 tsp.	5 ml
Sauce:		
Vegetable oil	2 tbsp.	30 ml
Butter	1 tbsp.	15 ml
Onion, chopped	1/2 cup	120 ml
Garlic clove, minced	1	1
Fish or chicken broth (see recipes, p. 41/39)	1/2 cup	120 ml
White wine	1/2 cup	120 ml
Tomatoes, peeled	1 cup	250 ml
Lemon juice	1/2 cup	120 ml
Flour	2 tbsp.	30 ml
Fresh parsley, chopped	1 tbsp.	15 ml
Salt and pepper, to taste		
Lemon, sliced (for garnish)	1	1

Combine all ingredients for the marinade. Add red snapper and marinate for 15 to 30 minutes. In a fry pan, heat oil and butter and sauté onion and garlic until golden. Add remaining ingredients and simmer over moderate heat for 10 minutes, stirring occasionally. Heat another fry pan and cook marinated snapper, covered, for 5 minutes on each side. Add the sauce and cook an additional 5 minutes, allowing sauce to reduce. Serve garnished with lemon slices.

Makes 4 servings.

Scorfano con Noci
Red Snapper with Walnuts

2 Red snappers, cleaned	1 lb. each	450 g
Flour	3 tbsp.	50 ml
Olive oil	1/4 cup	60 ml

Sauce:

Butter	3 tbsp.	50 ml
Green onions, chopped	1/2 cup	120 ml
Walnuts, coarsely chopped	1 cup	250 ml
Fish or chicken broth (see recipes, p. 41/39)	1/2 cup	120 ml
White wine	1/2 cup	120 ml
Brandy or Whiskey	1/4 cup	60 ml
Juice of 1 lemon		
Sage	1 pinch	1 pinch
Chopped parsley, to taste		
Salt and pepper, to taste		

In a fry pan, heat butter and sauté the onions and walnuts until lightly browned. Add remaining ingredients and simmer for 5 to 7 minutes, until sauce is reduced. In another fry pan, heat oil. Dredge red snapper in flour and cook in covered fry pan for 4 to 6 minutes on each side, or until tender. Add sauce and simmer an additional few minutes. Serve sprinkled with parsley.

Makes 4 servings.

Filetti di Sogliola con Avocado
Fillet of Sole with Avocado

Some of the sole available in North America is actually flounder. The best sole comes from Europe and is called Dover Sole or English Sole.

4 Sole fillets	6–8 oz. each	170–225g each

Marinade:

Olive oil	3 tbsp.	50 ml
Juice of 1 lemon		

Fresh parsley, chopped	1 tbsp.	15 ml
Dried sage	1 tsp.	5 ml
Salt and pepper, to taste		

Sauce:

Butter	3 tbsp.	50 ml
Flour	2 tbsp.	30 ml
Fish or chicken broth (see recipes, p. 41/39)	1/2 cup	120 ml
Red wine	1/2 cup	120 ml
35% cream	1/2 cup	120 ml
Brandy	1/4 cup	60 ml
Juice of 1 lemon		
Avocado, peeled and diced	1	1
Red pepper, chopped	1/2	1/2
Chopped parsley, to taste		
Salt and pepper, to taste		
Cucumber, sliced (for garnish)	1	1

Combine all ingredients for the marinade. Add the sole fillets and marinate for 15 to 30 minutes. To make sauce, heat the butter in a large skillet and stir in the flour to make a roux. Add the remaining sauce ingredients and simmer for a few minutes over moderate heat, stirring occasionally. Heat another fry pan. When hot, add the marinated fillets and marinade and cook, covered, for 4 minutes. Add the sauce, bring to a boil and serve. Garnish with cucumber slices, if desired.

Makes 4 servings.

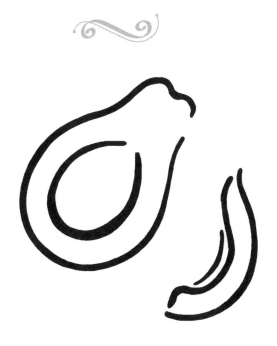

Bistecca di Pesce Spada al Vino Bianco
Swordfish Steak with White Wine Sauce

4 Swordfish steaks	5–6 oz. each	140–170 g each
Marinade:		
Olive oil	3 tbsp.	50 ml
Garlic clove, minced	1	1
Dried sage	1 tsp.	5 ml
White or black pepper	1/2 tsp.	2 ml
Sauce:		
Butter	2 tbsp.	30 ml
Small onion, chopped	1	1
Flour	1 tbsp.	15 ml
White wine	1/2 cup	120 ml
35% cream	1/3 cup	90 ml
Juice of 1 lemon		
Fresh parsley, chopped	2 tbsp.	30 ml
Salt and pepper, to taste		
Orange, sliced (for garnish)	1	1

Combine all ingredients for the marinade. Add sword fish and marinate for 15 to 30 minutes. For sauce: In a saucepan, heat butter and sauté the onion until translucent. Stir in the flour. Add remaining ingredients except parsley and orange. Simmer for 6 minutes over moderate heat, stirring occasionally. Heat another fry pan and cook marinated steaks, covered, for 2 minutes on each side. Add the sauce and parsley and simmer until fish is tender. Serve garnished with orange slices.

Makes 4 servings.

Eperlani con Vino e Pomodoro
Smelts Sautéed with Wine and Tomato Sauce

Smelts, cleaned	1 lb.	450 g
Flour	1/4 cup	60 ml
Olive oil	1/4 cup	60 ml
Sauce:		
Butter	2 tbsp.	30 ml
Onion, chopped	1/2 cup	120 ml
Garlic clove, minced	1	1
Fish or chicken broth (see recipes, p. 41/39)	1/2 cup	120 ml
White wine	1/2 cup	120 ml
Tomatoes, strained	1 cup	250 ml
Lemon juice	1/2 cup	120 ml
Oregano	1 pinch	1 pinch
Sage	1 pinch	1 pinch
Salt and pepper, to taste		

For sauce, Heat butter and sauté onion and garlic until translucent. Add remaining ingredients and simmer over moderate heat for 10 to 14 minutes, stirring occasionally. In another fry pan, heat oil. Dredge smelts in flour and sauté in pan for 2 to 3 minutes on each side. Add the sauce and simmer briefly.

Makes 4 servings.

Code d'Aragosta in Padella
Pan-Grilled Lobster Tails

Most of the lobster tails you buy are from the spiny or rock lobster, which lacks the claws of the better known North American homard lobster.

6 Lobster tails, cleaned	6 oz. each	170 g
Butter	1/4 cup	60 ml
Vegetable oil	1/4 cup	60 ml
Fish broth (see recipe, p. 41)	1/2 cup	120 ml
White wine	1/2 cup	120 ml
Lemon juice	3/4 cup	180 ml
Onion, chopped	1/2 cup	120 ml
Garlic, minced	3 tbsp.	50 ml
Fresh parsley, chopped	1/2 cup	120 ml
Aromatic preserve (see recipe, p. 17)	2 tbsp.	30 ml
Chili pepper preserve (see recipe, p. 18)	1 tbsp.	15 ml
Salt and pepper, to taste		

With a sharp knife, butterfly each lobster tail by splitting lengthwise through the top shell. In a large fry pan, heat butter and oil and add the lobster tails, flesh side down. Add all remaining ingredients and cover pan. Simmer until the lobster shells turn pink. Remove lobster and keep warm on a serving platter. Continue to cook the sauce until it reduces to one third. Serve the lobster, flesh side up and topped with the sauce.

Makes 6 servings.

Astice Americana Grigliata con Brandy e Burro
Pan-Grilled Lobster with Brandy and Butter

Large variety lobsters are called "astice."

4 fresh Lobsters	1 1/2 lbs. each	675 g each
Olive oil	1/3 cup	90 ml
Butter	1/3 cup	90 ml
Green onion, chopped	1 cup	250 ml
Garlic cloves, minced	4	4
White wine	1/2 cup	120 ml
Brandy	1/2 cup	120 ml

Aromatic preserve (see recipe, p. 17)	1/4 cup	60 ml
Lemon juice	3/4 cup	180 ml

To kill the lobsters, insert the tip of a knife into the back of each lobster, just behind the head. Split open each lobster lengthwise down the back. In a large skillet, heat oil and place lobsters, flesh side down in pan. Cover and cook until their shells turn pink, about 3 minutes on each side. Remove to a serving platter and keep warm until all lobsters are cooked. In the same skillet, melt butter and sauté onion and garlic until lightly browned. Lower heat to medium and return lobsters to the pan. Add wine, brandy and condiment and bring to a boil. Add lemon juice and serve piping hot.

Makes 4 servings.

Polpi al Pomodoro e Peperoni
Octopus with Red Pepper and Tomato Sauce

Larger varieties of octopus should be tenderized and skinned before cooking.

Octopus, cleaned	2 lbs.	900 g
Butter	2 tbsp.	30 ml
Olive oil	2 tbsp.	30 ml
Onion, chopped	1	1
Garlic cloves, minced	2	2
Red pepper, diced	1	1
Fish or chicken broth (see recipes, p. 41/39)	3/4 cup	180 ml
White wine	1/2 cup	120 ml
Lemon juice	1/2 cup	120 ml
Tomatoes, peeled	1 cup	250 ml
Fresh parsley, chopped	2 tbsp.	30 ml
Dried basil	1 tsp.	5 ml
Dried marjoram	1 tsp.	5 ml
Dried tarragon	1 tsp.	5 ml
Salt and pepper, to taste		

Bring a pot of water to a boil. Add octopus and cook for 15 minutes. Drain and cut into bite size pieces. In a medium saucepan, heat butter and oil. Sauté onion, garlic, pepper and octopus until lightly browned. Add remaining ingredients and cover pan. Simmer over moderate heat for 15 to 20 minutes, or until octopus is tender, stirring occasionally. Serve with some chopped parsley.

Makes 4 servings.

Ventagli Pettino con Funghi
Scallops with Oyster Mushrooms

Large scallops	2 lbs.	900 g
Olive oil	3 tbsp.	50 ml
Shallots, chopped	4	4
Garlic cloves, minced	3	3
Oyster mushrooms, sliced	2 cups	500 ml
Flour	2 tbsp.	30 ml
Butter	3 tbsp.	50 ml
35% cream or boiling milk	1 cup	250 ml
White wine or sherry	1/2 cup	120 ml
Lemon juice	1/2 cup	120 ml
Dried sage	1 tsp.	5 ml
Dried oregano	1 tsp.	5 ml
Dried basil or marjoram	1 tsp.	5 ml
Salt and pepper, to taste		

In a large fry pan, heat oil and sauté shallots, garlic and mushrooms for 3 to 4 minutes, stirring frequently. Add scallops and cover pan. Continue cooking over moderate heat until scallops are firm. Stir in flour and butter. Add remaining ingredients and stir until sauce thickens.

Makes 4 servings.

Gamberoni Grigliati con Oregano e Aglio
Grilled Tiger Shrimp with Oregano and Garlic

Tiger shrimp, butterflied and de-veined	2 lbs.	900 g

Marinade:

Olive oil	1/4 cup	60 ml
Garlic cloves, minced	2	2
Fresh parsley, chopped	1/4 cup	60 ml
Dried oregano	1 tsp.	5 ml

Sauce:

Butter	3 tbsp.	50 ml
Onion, chopped	1	1
Flour	1 tbsp.	15 ml

Fish or chicken broth (see recipes, p. 41/39)	1 cup	250 ml
White wine	1/2 cup	120 ml
Tomatoes, strained	1/2 cup	120 ml
35% cream or boiling milk	1/2 cup	120 ml
Salt and pepper, to taste		

Combine all ingredients for the marinade. Add shrimp and marinate for 15 to 30 minutes. For sauce, heat butter in a fry pan and sauté onion until golden. Stir in the flour. Add remaining ingredients and simmer for 6 minutes, stirring occasionally. Heat another fry pan and cook marinated shrimp, covered, until pink. Add the sauce and simmer briefly.

Makes 4 servings.

Calamari con Prosciutto e Pomodoro
Squid with Prosciutto and Tomato Sauce

Squid is a very tasty and chewy meat. Its ink is sometimes used to colour pastas and sauces.

Small squid, cleaned	2 lbs.	900 g
Olive oil	3 tbsp.	50 ml

Sauce:

Butter	2 tbsp.	30 ml
Olive oil	1 tbsp.	15 ml
Onion, chopped	1/2 cup	120 ml
Garlic cloves, minced	2	2
Green pepper, diced	1/2 cup	120 ml
Prosciutto, chopped	4 oz.	115 g
Fish or chicken broth	3/4 cup	180 ml
(see recipes, p. 41/39)		
White wine	1/2 cup	120 ml
Tomatoes, strained	1 cup	250 ml
Crushed peppercorn	1 tsp.	5 ml
Salt and pepper, to taste		

To make sauce, heat butter and oil in a fry pan. Sauté onion, garlic, green pepper, and prosciutto until onions are translucent. Add remaining ingredients and simmer over moderate heat for 10 to 14 minutes, stirring occasionally. In another fry pan, heat oil and cook squid, covered, over high heat for 5 to 6 minutes, or until tender. Add sauce and simmer an additional few minutes.

Makes 4 servings.

Poultry and Game

Chicken has always been and is still considered somewhat of a delicacy in Italy. It is taken a bit for granted here in North America because it is so readily available and economical, but it is still one of the most delicious meats available.

Buying Poultry

Whenever possible, you should buy your poultry and game fresh. If you must buy it frozen, make sure there is no frost or ice on the outside of the package and that the bird is completely hard. Always defrost your bird slowly in the refrigerator. for a large turkey, this may take 2 to 3 days, but the meat will have a better taste and consistency.

When you are buying fresh, the meat should be from a young bird. To test for freshness, press on the breastbone. If it is soft, the bird is young and the meat will be moist and tender. The best tasting poultry meat comes from free-range birds. Refrigerate the bird immediately and make sure you don't let it sit at room temperature for more than a 1/2 hour.

If you require chicken parts for a recipe, it is more economical to buy a whole chicken and cut it yourself. You will save money and any additional parts can be saved for soup stock, so no part of the bird is wasted.

Cutting Poultry

First of all, wash your hands before and after you handle raw poultry. Secondly, be sure you thoroughly wash and dry the bird, inside and out.

To section the bird, pull the thighs from the body and with a sharp boning knife, slice through the joint. Tear the thighs from the body and slice through the skin, if necessary. At this point, you may separate the thighs from the drumsticks by slicing through the knee joint.

Place the bird breast up and cut down the center of the breastbone. Cut away the breast meat on either side by scraping with your knife between the ribcage and the meat. When the breasts have been separated, remove the skin and the small bone. At this point, you may separate the wings from the breasts by slicing through the shoulder joint. So, now your bird is divided into either 4 or 8 sections and is ready to cook.

Piccata di Pollo con Rosmarino e Vino
Chicken Piccata with Rosemary and Wine

This dish makes a nice accompaniment to noodles in cream sauce.

Chicken breasts, skinned and de-boned	4	4
Flour	3 tbsp.	50 ml
Eggs, beaten	2	2
Olive oil	3 tbsp.	50 ml
Sauce:		
Butter	2 tbsp.	30 ml
Onion, chopped	1	1
Flour	1 tbsp.	15 ml
Chicken broth (see recipe, p. 39)	1 cup	250 ml
White wine	1/2 cup	120 ml
Fresh parsley, chopped	2 tbsp.	30 ml
Dried rosemary	1 tsp.	5 ml
Salt and pepper, to taste		

To make the sauce, heat butter in a fry pan and sauté onion until translucent. Stir in the flour. Add remaining ingredients and simmer over moderate heat for 6 minutes, stirring occasionally. In another fry pan heat the oil. Dredge chicken breasts in flour and dip in eggs. Sauté in fry pan for 4 minutes on each side, or until tender. Add the sauce and simmer for a few minutes.

Makes 4 servings.

Supreme di Pollo Giardiniera
Garden-Style Chicken Suprèmes

A supreme is a breast of chicken with the wing joint still attached.

6 Chicken suprèmes, lightly pounded	7 oz. each	200 g each
Olive oil	1/3 cup	90 ml
Flour	2 tbsp.	30 ml
Mushrooms, sliced	1 cup	250 ml
Red pepper, julienned	1 cup	250 ml
Leeks, white part, julienned	1 cup	250 ml
Garlic clove, minced	1	1

Risotto is an Italian favourite. Shown here is Risotto with Sun-Dried Tomato and Porcini Mushroom (page 51).

Polenta is a delicious accompaniment to a meal. It can be served directly from the pot as "soft polenta", or cooled in a pan and sliced.

Penne alla Rustica. Large tubes of pasta with
mushrooms, green peppers and olives (page 82).

Spaghetti with Mussels and Tomato Sauce (page 74)

Pan-Grilled Lobster Tails (page 98) with white wine and herbs.

Halibut Steaks with Shallots and Mushrooms (page 88).

Shrimp with Wine and Tomato Sauce, or with Smelts (page 97).

Chicken broth (see recipe, p. 39)	1/2 cup	120 ml
White wine	1/2 cup	120 ml
10% cream, boiled	1/2 cup	120 ml
Tomatoes, peeled and chopped	1 cup	250 ml
Salt and pepper, to taste		

In a large fry pan, heat oil. Dredge the chicken supremes in flour and cook for 3 minutes on each side. Remove from heat and set aside. Combine mushrooms, peppers and leeks in fry pan and sauté for 4 minutes. Return chicken to the pan and add remaining ingredients. Cover and simmer over moderate heat for 10 minutes, stirring occasionally.

Makes 6 servings.

Petti di Pollo con Olive
Chicken Breasts with Olives

Olive oil	1/3 cup	85 ml
Garlic cloves, thinly sliced	2	2
Flour	3 tbsp.	45 ml
Chicken breasts, deboned, with skin on	4	4
White wine	1 cup	250 ml
Juice of 1/2 lemon		
Parsley	1 tsp.	5 ml
Whole peppercorns	1tbsp.	15 ml
Oregano	1/2 tsp.	3 ml
Black olives, pitted	1 cup	250 ml
Anchovy fillets	3	3
Salt and pepper	to taste	

In large frying pan, heat olive oil and sauté garlic until soft. Dredge chicken in flour, then pan-fry for 5 minutes each side until browned. Remove chicken from pan. Add all remaining ingredients to pan and sauté for a few minutes. Lower heat to medium, place chicken back in pan, cover and simmer for 5 minutes.

Serves 4.

Scaloppine di Pollo alla Marsala
Chicken Scallopini with Marsala

6 Chicken breasts	4 oz. each	115 g each
Flour	1/4 cup	60 ml
Vegetable oil	1/3 cup	90 ml
Butter	3 tbsp.	50 ml
Green onions, chopped	1/2 cup	120 ml
Mushrooms, sliced	2 cups	500 ml
Chicken stock (see recipe, p. 40)	1 cup	250 ml
Marsala wine	1/2 cup	120 ml
Fresh parsley, chopped	2 tbsp.	30 ml
Salt and pepper, to taste		

In a large fry pan, heat oil and butter. Dredge the chicken breasts in flour and cook for 2 minutes on each side. Add onions and mushrooms and cook for 4 minutes, stirring occasionally. Lower heat to medium and add remaining ingredients. Simmer until liquid reduces slightly and thickens.

Makes 4 to 6 servings.

Involtini di Pollo con Salsa di Funghi
Chicken Roulade with Mushroom Sauce

6 Chicken breasts, butterflied and pounded	6 oz. each	170 g each
Pancetta, thinly sliced	12 slices	12 slices
Mozzarella, cut into six strips	3 oz	85 g
Red pepper, sliced into 6 strips	1	1
Flour	1/4 cup	60 ml
Vegetable oil	5 tbsp.	75 ml
Onion, chopped	1 cup	250 ml
Mushrooms, sliced	12	12
Gravy (see recipe, p. 23)	1 1/2 cups	375 ml
White wine	3/4 cup	180 ml
Aromatic preserve (see recipe, p. 17)	2 tbsp.	30 ml
Salt and pepper, to taste		

Spread the flattened chicken breasts on wax paper. Using 1 tbsp. (15 ml) of the flour, lightly dust the tops.In the center of each, place 2 slices of pancetta, 1 strip of mozzarella, and 1 strip of pepper. Roll each one tightly and dredge in remaining flour. In a large fry pan, heat oil and cook the roulades for 2 minutes on each side or until golden. Lower heat to medium and add onions and mushrooms. Cover and cook for 4 minutes, stirring occasionally. Add remaining ingredients and bring to a boil before serving.

Makes 6 servings.

Filetti di Tacchino con Funghi e Crema
Turkey Fillets with Mushroom and Cream Sauce

6 Turkey breast cutlets, pounded	8 oz. each	225 g each
Vegetable oil	1/4 cup	60 ml
Butter	1/4 cup	60 ml
Shallots, chopped	3	3
Garlic clove, minced	1	1
Mushrooms, sliced	6	6
Flour	2 tbsp.	30 ml
Chicken or turkey broth (see recipes, p. 39/40)	1/2 cup	120 ml
White wine	1/2 cup	120 ml
35% cream	1/2 cup	120 ml
Fresh parsley, chopped	2 tbsp.	30 ml
Salt and pepper, to taste		

To make the sauce, heat butter in a saucepan and sauté shallots, garlic and mushrooms until lightly browned. Stir in flour and cook for 2 minutes. Add remaining ingredients, except parsley, and simmer over moderate heat for 6 minutes, stirring occasionally. In another fry pan, heat oil and sauté the turkey fillets for 4 minutes on each side, or until cooked through. Add sauce and parsley and simmer briefly before serving.

Makes 6 servings.

Bistecca di Tacchino Grigliata in Padella
Pan-Grilled Turkey Steaks

4 Turkey breast steaks, pounded 1/2 inch (1 cm) thick	8 oz. each	225 g each
Vegetable oil	1/4 cup	60 ml
Butter	1/4 cup	60 ml
Green onions, chopped	1 cup	250 ml
Red pepper, diced	1/2 cup	120 ml
Chicken or turkey stock (see recipes, p. 40)	1/2 cup	120 ml
White wine	1/2 cup	120 ml
Aromatic preserve (see recipe, p. 17)	2 tbsp.	30 ml
Salt and pepper, to taste		

In a large skillet, heat oil and butter and sauté turkey steaks for 2 minutes on each side. Add onion and pepper and sauté for 3 minutes. Lower heat to medium and add remaining ingredients. Simmer for 5 minutes, turning the turkey steaks over occasionally until done.

Makes 4 servings.

Cornovaglia alla Paesana
Cornish Hens Country Style

2 Cornish hens, split in half	1 lb. each	450 g each
Vegetable oil	1/2 cup	120 ml
Onion, chopped	1 cup	250 ml
Garlic cloves, minced	2	2
Pepper, diced	1/2 cup	120 ml
Mushrooms, sliced	2 cups	500 ml
Chicken stock (see recipe, p. 40)	1 cup	250 ml
Tomatoes, peeled and chopped	1 cup	250 ml
White wine	1/2 cup	120 ml
Aromatic preserve (see recipe, p. 17)	2 tbsp.	30 ml
Salt and pepper, to taste		

In a large skillet, heat oil and cook hens for 6 minutes on each side. Add onion, garlic, pepper and mushrooms and sauté for 8 minutes, or until hens and vegetables are tender. Lower heat to medium and add remaining ingredients. Cover and simmer until the meat comes away easily from the bones.

Makes 4 servings.

Arrosto di Pollo
Roast Chicken

2 Roasting chickens	3 lbs. each	1.3 kg each
Marinade:		
Vegetable oil	1/2 cup	120 ml
Lemon juice	1/2 cup	120 ml
Balsamic vinegar	1/2 cup	120 ml
Dried rosemary	2 tbsp.	30 ml
Dried sage	2 tbsp.	30 ml
Dried oregano	2 tbsp.	30 ml
Ginger powder	2 tbsp.	30 ml
Bacon strips, chopped	4	4
Salt and pepper, to taste		
Sauce:		
Chicken broth (see recipe, p. 39)	1 quart	1 litre
Butter, melted	3/4 cup	180 ml
All-purpose flour	1/4 cup	60 ml
White wine	1 cup	250 ml

Preheat your oven to 475°F (245°C). Combine all ingredients for the marinade. Place the chickens in a large roasting pan and pour marinade over them, rubbing the seasonings into the skin. Place in oven and roast for 35 minutes. Add the broth and continue cooking for another 35 minutes, basting occasionally. To check if meat is cooked, prick the leg with a fork and if the juices run clear, the chicken is done. Remove to a serving platter and keep warm. Skim the fat off the roasting juices. Strain the roasting liquid into a saucepan and bring to a boil. Mix the flour into the melted butter, making sure no lumps remain. Add to the boiling broth, stirring well. Add the wine and simmer for 20 minutes, stirring occasionally. The sauce should thicken into a gravy-like consistency. Serve in a small bowl alongside the chickens.

Serves 6 to 8 people.

Arrosto di Tacchino
Roast Turkey

If you are roasting a whole turkey, double the quantities.

Turkey half	7–8 lbs.	3–3.5 kg
Marinade:		
Vegetable oil	1/2 cup	120 ml
Lemon juice	1/2 cup	120 ml
Garlic cloves, chopped	4	4
Bacon strips, chopped	2	2
Juniper berries, crushed	1/4 cup	60 ml
Dry mustard	1/4 cup	60 ml
Dried sage	2 tbsp.	30 ml
Ginger powder	2 tbsp.	30 ml
Salt and pepper, to taste		
Sauce:		
Chicken or turkey broth (see recipes, p. 39/40)	1 quart	1 litre
White wine	1/2 cup	120 ml
Sherry or Marsala wine	1/2 cup	120 ml
Soy sauce	1/4 cup	60 ml
Butter, melted or olive oil	1/2 cup	120 ml
All-purpose flour	1/4 cup	60 ml

Preheat your oven to 500°F (260°C). Combine all ingredients for the marinade. Place turkey in a large roasting pan and pour marinade over it, rubbing the seasonings into the skin. Place in oven and roast for 50 minutes. Lower the oven temperature to 400°F (205°C) and add the broth, wine, sherry and soy sauce. Continue to cook for another 50 minutes, basting occasionally. When turkey is done, remove to a serving platter and keep warm. Strain the roasting juices into a medium pot and bring to a boil. Mix the flour into the melted butter, making sure all lumps are removed. Stir into the boiling broth and simmer over medium heat for 10 to 15 minutes, stirring frequently. Serve in a bowl alongside the roast turkey.

Serves 6 to 8 people.

Arrosto di Papera

Roast Duckling

2 Ducklings	3–4 lbs. each	1.5 kg each
Marinade:		
Vegetable oil	1/2 cup	120 ml
Corn syrup or liquid honey	1/2 cup	120 ml
Lemon juice	1/2 cup	120 ml
Onion, diced	1	1
Garlic cloves, chopped	4	4
Dried rosemary	2 tbsp.	30 ml
The peel of 2 oranges, chopped		
Salt and pepper, to taste		
Sauce:		
Orange juice	2 cups	500 ml
Chicken broth (see recipe, p. 39)	2 cups	500 ml
White wine	1/2 cup	120 ml
Cornstarch or potato flour	1/4 cup	60 ml
Oranges, sliced (for garnish)	2	2

Preheat your oven to 500°F (260°C). Combine all ingredients for the marinade. Place ducklings in a large roasting pan and pour marinade over them, rubbing the seasonings into the skin. Place in oven and roast for 45 minutes. Lower heat to 400°F (205°C) and add orange juice and broth. Continue to cook for about 1 hour, basting occasionally.

Tip: If the meat on the leg comes away easily from the bone, the ducklings are done.

When done, remove to a serving platter and keep warm. Skim the fat off the roasting juices. Strain the roasting liquid into a saucepan and bring to a boil. Dissolve the cornstarch in the wine and pour into the boiling broth, mixing well. Simmer for 5 minutes until slightly thickened. (This should give you about 4 cups/1 litre of sauce.) Serve sauce in a gravy dish and garnish the ducklings with orange slices.

Serves 6 to 8 people.

Meat Dishes

Beef

When buying beef, you should pay attention to the fat. The more fat there is, the more tender the meat will be. The fat should be white and crumbly. If the fat is yellowish, the meat will likely be sinewy or tough.

Broiling and Grilling

These are healthy methods of cooking your beef that allow you to cut back on excess fat. The best cuts for broiling or grilling steaks are filet mignon, and any loin cut – club, porterhouse, and T-bone. Be sure when you are cooking that the heat is high enough to sear the meat and seal in the juices. and never pierce the meat while cooking or the juices will escape. Turn the cuts over with a pair of tongs.

Pan-frying is also an effective and healthy way to cook steak, provided you use a non-stick skillet which requires no extra oil or fat.

Roasting

The best cut for roast beef is a prime rib roast. You can also use a good top or bottom sirloin, or the eye of the round, if sliced thinly when served.

For pot roasts, less expensive cuts like chuck, brisket, and rump can be used. Soaking these cuts in a marinade will make them more tender and tasty. and never pierce your meat while roasting, or the juices will run out, leaving you with a dry roast. If you follow my method for cooking roasts, you'll have tender, moist meat every time.

Carving

After your beef is properly cooked, you must ensure that the meat remains juicy and tender by carving correctly. Remember that you must always cut across the grain. When carving a roast, you should carve it so that the juices run back into the remaining meat and not onto the plate.

Filetto di Manzo Grigliato con Funghi
Pan-Grilled Filet Mignon with Oyster Mushrooms

4 Beef tenderloin fillets	6–8 oz. each	170–225 g each
Olive oil	2 tbsp.	30 ml
Butter	3 tbsp.	50 ml
Shallots, chopped	4	4
Garlic clove, minced	1	1
Oyster mushrooms	2 cups	500 ml
Tomato paste	1 tbsp.	15 ml
Beef stock (see recipe, p. 43)	3/4 cup	180 ml
Red wine	1/2 cup	120 ml
Fresh parsley, chopped	2 tbsp.	30 ml
Salt and pepper, to taste		

In a large fry pan, heat oil and add fillets. Cover pan and brown fillets for 2 minutes on each side. Add butter, shallots, garlic and mushrooms and sauté for 3 to 4 minutes, turning the fillets often. Lower heat to medium. Dilute tomato paste with stock and wine, adding parsley, salt and pepper. Add to pan and simmer for 4 minutes.

Makes 4 servings.

Medaglione di Filetto di Manzo con Gorgonzola
Medallion of Beef Tenderloin with Gorgonzola Cheese

Beef tenderloin tips, lightly pounded	1.5 lbs.	675 g
Olive oil	3 tbsp.	50 ml
Butter	2 tbsp.	30 ml
Shallots, chopped	3	3
Garlic clove, minced	1	1
Celery stalk, chopped	1	1
Gorgonzola or blue cheese, diced	1 cup	250 ml
35% cream	1/2 cup	120 ml
Beef broth (see recipe, p. 42)	1/2 cup	120 ml
White wine	1/2 cup	120 ml
Brandy or vodka	1/4 cup	60 ml
Salt and pepper, to taste		

In a large fry pan, heat oil and butter. Add beef medallions and brown for 2 minutes on each side. Add shallots, garlic and celery and cook, covered, for 2 minutes. Add remaining ingredients. Lower heat to medium and simmer for 5 minutes, stirring occasionally.

Makes 4 servings.

Medaglione di Filetto di Manzo alla Cacciatora
Beef Tenderloin Hunter Style

Alla cacciatora, *or "hunter style" refers to a dish made with sautéed and braised meats, often served with wild mushrooms and tomato sauce.*

Beef tenderloin, 1/2-inch (1-cm) thick slices	2 lbs.	900 g
Flour	3 tbsp.	50 ml
Butter	1/4 cup	60 ml
Sauce:		
Olive oil	1/4 cup	60 ml
Onion, diced	1 cup	250 ml
Bell pepper, sliced	1 cup	250 ml
Mushrooms, sliced	2 cups	500 ml
Garlic cloves, minced	2	2
Beef stock (see recipe, p. 43)	1 cup	250 ml
Tomatoes, strained	1 cup	250 ml
Red wine	1 cup	250 ml
Chili pepper preserve (see recipe, p. 18)	1 tbsp.	15 ml
Salt and pepper, to taste		

To make the sauce, heat oil in a fry pan and sauté onion, pepper, mushrooms and garlic for 5 minutes, stirring occasionally. Add remaining ingredients, lower heat to medium and simmer for 10 minutes. In another fry pan, heat butter. Dredge the beef slices in flour and brown in the pan for 2 minutes on each side. Add the sauce and simmer for a few minutes before serving.

Makes 4 to 6 servings

Bistecca di Manzo al Pepe
Pepper Steak

4 Beef loin steaks	6–8 oz. each	170–225 g each
Crushed peppercorn	2 tbsp.	30 ml
Marinade:		
Olive oil	3 tbsp.	50 ml
Dry mustard	1 tsp.	5 ml
Sauce:		
Butter	2 tbsp.	30 ml
Onion, finely chopped	1	1
Flour	1 tbsp.	15 ml
Beef broth (see recipe, p. 42)	1 cup	250 ml
Red wine	1/2 cup	120 ml
35% cream	1/2 cup	120 ml
Brandy	1/4 cup	60 ml
Hot pepper sauce	3 drops	3 drops
Paprika	1 tbsp.	15 ml
Fresh parsley, chopped	2 tbsp.	30 ml
Salt and pepper, to taste		

Combine ingredients for the marinade. Add steaks and marinate for 15 to 30 minutes. Press in peppercorn. In a fry pan, heat butter and sauté onion until golden. Stir in flour. Add remaining ingredients and simmer over moderate heat for 8 to 10 minutes, stirring frequently. Heat a large skillet and add marinated steaks. Cover and cook for 4 to 5 minutes on each side. Add the sauce and simmer for 2 to 3 minutes before serving.

Makes 4 servings.

Paiarda di Lombo di Manzo alla Baronessa
Paillard of Beef Strip Loin Baroness Style

A paillard is a thinly pounded piece of meat that is usually grilled or sautéed.

6 Strip loin steaks, butterflied and pounded	8 oz. each	225 g each
Aromatic preserve (see recipe, p. 17)	3 tbsp.	50 ml
Olive oil	5 tbsp.	75 ml

Shallots, chopped	1 cup	250 ml
Flour	1 tbsp.	15 ml
Beef stock (see recipe, p. 43)	1/2 cup	120 ml
Red wine	1/2 cup	120 ml
35% cream	3/4 cup	180 ml
Dry mustard	2 tbsp.	30 ml
Salt and pepper, to taste		

Marinate the steaks in the aromatic preserve for 2 hours. In a fry pan, heat oil and sauté the shallots for 3 minutes. Stir in the flour. Add remaining ingredients and simmer over moderate heat for 7 minutes, stirring occasionally. Heat a large fry pan and cook marinated steaks for 2 minutes on each side. Add the sauce and bring to a boil before serving.

Makes 6 servings.

Costatine di Manzo al Forno
Baked Short Ribs of Beef

Short ribs of beef	4 lbs.	1.8 kg
Aromatic preserve (see recipe, p. 17)	2 tbsp.	30 ml
Celery, diced	2 cups	500 ml
Carrots, diced	2 cups	500 ml
Onion, diced	1 cup	250 ml
Bell pepper, diced	1/2 cup	120 ml
Potatoes, peeled and quartered	4	4
Tomatoes, chopped	2 cups	500 ml
Beef stock (see recipe, p. 43)	2 quarts	2 litres
Red wine	1 cup	250 ml
Garlic, minced	2 tbsp.	30 ml
Salt and pepper, to taste		

Preheat your oven to 450°F (230°C). Combine short ribs with the aromatic preserve; mix well. Place ribs in a roasting pan and cover. Cook for 40 minutes, stirring occasionally. Lower heat to 400°F (205°C) and add remaining ingredients. Continue cooking for another hour and ten minutes, or until the ribs are tender.

Makes 4 servings.

Braciola di Manzo al Vino
Ground Beef Steak with Wine

Lean ground beef	2 lbs.	900 g
Onions, finely chopped	1 cup	250 ml
Eggs	3	3
Bread crumbs	1/2 cup	120 ml
Dry mustard	2 tbsp.	30 ml
Aromatic preserve (see recipe, p. 17)	2 tbsp.	30 ml
Salt and pepper, to taste		
Vegetable oil	1/4 cup	60 ml
Gravy (see recipe, p. 23)	2 cups	500 ml
Red wine	1/2 cup	120 ml

In a large bowl, combine beef, onions, eggs, bread crumbs, and seasonings. Mix thoroughly by hand. Divide the mixture into 8 portions and flatten into ovals, about the size of hamburgers.In a large fry pan, heat oil and fry steaks for 4 minutes on each side. Add the gravy and wine and bring to a boil.

Makes 8 servings.

Stufato di Manzo
Beef Stew

Lean beef, shoulder cut, cubed	3 lbs.	1.4 kg
Flour	2 tbsp.	30 ml
Vegetable oil	1/4 cup	60 ml
Onion, diced	1 cup	250 ml
Celery, diced	1 cup	250 ml
Carrots, diced	1 cup	250 ml
Garlic clove, minced	1	1
Beef broth (see recipe, p. 42)	1 quart	1 litre
Red wine	1 cup	250 ml
Tomatoes, diced	1 cup	250 ml
Aromatic preserve (see recipe, p. 17)	2 tbsp.	30 ml
Salt and pepper, to taste		

In a large saucepan, heat oil. Dredge the cubed beef in flour and sauté until browned on every side. Add vegetables and garlic and cook for 6 minutes, stirring occasionally. Lower heat to medium and add remaining ingredients. Cover and simmer until meat is tender, about 1 hour, stirring occasionally.

Makes 4 to 6 servings.

Polpettone in Padella
Meatloaf Casserole

Finely ground beef and veal	2 lbs.	900 g
Eggs	4	4
Vegetable oil	1/3 cup	90 ml
Bread crumbs	1 cup	250 ml
Cooked ham, chopped	3/4 cup	180 ml
Parmesan cheese, grated	1/2 cup	120 ml
Flour	1/4 cup	60 ml
Garlic cloves, minced	4	4
Fresh parsley, chopped	1/4 cup	60 ml
Dried basil	1 tbsp.	15 ml
Salt and pepper, to taste		
Hard-boiled eggs	8	8
Sauce:		
Beef stock (see p. 43)	1 quart	1 litre
Red wine	1/2 cup	120 ml
Tomato paste	1/4 cup	60 ml

To make meatballs, combine all ingredients, except hard-boiled eggs, in a large bowl. Mix thoroughly and divide mixture into four equal parts. Place each on a piece of oiled aluminum foil and flatten to a 1-inch (2.5-cm) thickness. Place two hard-boiled eggs in the center of each section and mould the meat around the eggs. Wrap each loaf in foil. Place all four loaves in a large heated skillet. Dilute the tomato paste with the wine and stock and place in a skillet. Cover and simmer over moderate heat for 50 minutes to 1 hour. When the loaves are cooked, remove the foil and slice horizontally on a serving platter. Serve with remaining sauce.

Makes 4 servings.

Veal

Top quality veal comes from calves about three months old that have been milk-fed. This produces pale, tender meat. Darker meat, which is pink in colour, comes from slightly older calves that have been allowed to eat grass. This baby beef is called vitellone.

Since veal comes from a young animal, it has little fat and no marbling, and therefore should be cooked for as short a time as possible to ensure that it does not get dry and tough. Most recipes call for it to be pounded thinly and cooked quickly or braised in liquid.

Veal cutlets, scaloppine and paillard are all leg cuts. The best cut is from the inside of the thigh, called *fesa di vitello*.

To pound a piece of veal, lay the leg cut on a cutting board. with a sharp knife, cut a slice about as thick as your finger by carving across the grain of the meat. Lay the cutlet between sheets of plastic wrap and pound with a meat hammer until thin.

Cotolette di Vitello alla Parmigiana
Breaded Veal Cutlets Parma Style

In Italy, "alla parmigiana" means "Parma style," but in North America, if refers to something breaded, fried, topped with tomato sauce and cheese, and baked.

6 Veal cutlets, pounded	4 oz. each	115 g each
Flour	1/4 cup	60 ml
Eggs, beaten	3	3
Milk	1/3 cup	90 ml
Salt and pepper, to taste		
Breadcrumbs	3 cups	750 ml
Vegetable oil	1 cup	250 ml
Tomato sauce (see recipe, p. 27)	2 cups	500 ml
Mozzarella cheese, sliced	1 lb.	450 g

Place three bowls on your counter. In one bowl, place flour. In the second bowl, combine beaten eggs, milk, salt and pepper. In the third bowl, place breadcrumbs. Dredge the cutlets in flour first, dip them in the egg mixture, then dredge them in the breadcrumbs, making sure they are entirely covered. In a large fry pan, heat the oil. Fry cutlets until they are golden brown on each side. Then place the cutlets in a large baking dish and top with the tomato sauce and cheese. Bake in a pre-heated 400°F (205°C) oven or under a broiler until the cheese is melted.

Tip: This same method of preparing cutlets can also be used for pork, chicken, or turkey.

Makes 6 servings.

Filetto di Vitello con Piselli
Veal Tenderloin with Peas

Veal fillet, cut lengthwise into 4 slices and pounded	1 lb.	450 g

Marinade:

Olive oil	1/4 cup	60 ml
Garlic clove, minced	1	1
Dry mustard	1 tbsp.	15 ml
Dried sage	1 tsp.	5 ml
Crushed peppercorn	1 tsp.	5 ml

Sauce:

Butter	2 tbsp.	30 ml
Onion, chopped	1/2 cup	120 ml
Red pepper, sliced	1	1
Frozen peas	1/2 cup	120 ml
Chicken broth (see recipe, p. 39)	1/2 cup	120 ml
White wine	1/2 cup	120 ml
Tomatoes, peeled or strained	1 cup	250 ml
35% cream	1/2 cup	120 ml
The peel of 1/2 an orange, chopped		
Salt and pepper, to taste		

Combine all ingredients for the marinade. Add veal slices and marinate for 30 minutes. To make the sauce, heat butter in a fry pan and sauté onion until translucent. Add remaining ingredients, except cream. Simmer over moderate heat for 8 to 10 minutes, stirring occasionally. Heat another fry pan and add marinated fillets. Cover and cook for 3 to 4 minutes on each side. Add the sauce and the cream and simmer a few minutes before serving.

Makes 4 servings.

Medaglione di Vitello con Asparagi
Veal Medallions with Asparagus

8 Medallions of veal, pounded	3 oz. each	85 g each
Marinade:		
Olive oil	1/4 cup	60 ml
Dried sage	1/2 tsp.	2 ml
Crushed peppercorn	1 tsp.	5 ml
Sauce:		
Olive oil	2 tbsp.	30 ml
Butter	2 tbsp.	30 ml
Shallots, chopped	1 cup	250 ml
Garlic clove, minced	1	1
Asparagus tips	2 cups	500 ml
Flour	1 tbsp.	15 ml
Chicken broth (see recipe, p. 39)	1/2 cup	120 ml
White wine	1/2 cup	120 ml
35% cream	1/2 cup	120 ml
Salt and pepper, to taste		

Combine ingredients for the marinade. Add veal medallions and marinate for 30 minutes. To make the sauce, heat oil and butter in a fry pan. Sauté shallots, garlic, and asparagus until lightly browned. Stir in the flour. Add remaining ingredients and simmer over moderate heat for 4 minutes, stirring occasionally. Heat another fry pan and add marinated medallions. Cover and cook for 2 minutes on each side. Add the sauce and simmer for a few minutes before serving.

Makes 4 servings.

Medaglione di Vitello con Melanzana e Crema
Veal Medallions with Eggplant and Cream Sauce

6 Veal cutlets, pounded	3 oz. each	85 g each
Marinade:		
Olive oil	3 tbsp.	50 ml
Dried oregano	1 tsp.	5 ml
Crushed peppercorn	1 tsp.	5 ml

Sauce:

Olive oil	2 tbsp.	30 ml
Butter	2 tbsp.	30 ml
Onion, chopped	1/2 cup	120 ml
Eggplant, peeled and diced	1	1
Flour	1 tbsp.	15 ml
Chicken broth (see recipe, p. 39)	3/4 cup	180 ml
35% cream or boiling milk	1/2 cup	120 ml
Parmesan or Mozzarella, grated	3 tbsp.	50 ml

Combine ingredients for the marinade. Add veal cutlets and marinate for 30 minutes. To make the sauce, heat oil and butter in a fry pan. Sauté the onion and eggplant until lightly browned. Stir in the flour. Add remaining ingredients, except cheese, and simmer over moderate heat for 4 to 6 minutes, stirring occasionally. Heat another fry pan and add marinated veal. Cover and cook for 2 minutes on each side. Add the sauce and cheese and simmer, covered, until cheese is melted.

Makes 6 servings.

Costolette di Vitello in Padella alla Pizzaiola
Pan-Grilled Veal Chops with Tomato and Oregano Sauce

6 Lean veal chops	6 oz. each	170 g each
Flour	3 tbsp.	50 ml
Vegetable oil	1/3 cup	90 ml
Onion, chopped	1/2 cup	120 ml
Garlic clove, minced	1	1
Tomatoes, peeled and chopped	2 cups	500 ml
Stuffed olives, chopped	1 cup	250 ml
White wine	3/4 cup	180 ml
Dried oregano	2 tbsp.	30 ml
Salt and pepper, to taste		

In a large fry pan, heat oil. Dredge the veal chops in flour and sauté for 3 minutes on each side. Add the onion and garlic and sauté for 2 minutes. Lower the heat to medium and add remaining ingredients. Cover and cook for 12 minutes, stirring occasionally.

Makes 6 servings.

Veal Piccata Galante
Veal Piccata with Mushrooms and Green Pepper

8 Slices of lean veal, pounded	4 oz. each	115 g each
Flour	3 tbsp.	50 ml
Eggs, beaten	3	3
Olive oil	3 tbsp.	50 ml
Sauce:		
Butter	2 tbsp.	30 ml
Green onion, chopped	1 cup	250 ml
Green pepper, diced	1 cup	250 ml
Mushrooms, sliced	2 cups	500 ml
Artichoke hearts, sliced	2 cups	500 ml
Chicken broth (see recipe, p. 39)	1/2 cup	120 ml
White wine	1/2 cup	120 ml
Salt and pepper, to taste		

To make the sauce, heat butter in a skillet, and sauté onions, peppers and mushrooms until lightly browned. Add remaining ingredients and simmer over moderate heat for 5 minutes, stirring occasionally. In another fry pan, heat oil. Dredge each veal slice in flour and then dip in beaten eggs. Sauté slices for 2 minutes on each side, or until golden. Add sauce and simmer briefly before serving.

Makes 4 servings.

Bistecca di Vitello con Funghi
Veal Flank Steak with Mushroom Sauce

2 Veal flank steaks, tenderized	8–10 oz. each	225–285 g each
Marinade:		
Olive oil	1/4 cup	60 ml
Dried sage	1 tsp.	5 ml
White or black pepper	1/2 tsp.	2 ml
Sauce:		
Olive oil	1 tbsp.	15 ml
Onion, chopped	1/2	1/2
Garlic clove, minced	1	1
Large mushrooms, sliced	6	6

Flour	1 tbsp.	15 ml
Beef or chicken broth (see recipes, p. 42/39)	1/2 cup	120 ml
Red wine	1/2 cup	120 ml
Tomato paste	1 tbsp.	15 ml
Fresh parsley, chopped	2 tbsp.	30 ml
Salt and pepper, to taste		

Combine ingredients for the marinade. Add veal steaks and marinate for 30 minutes. To make the sauce, heat oil in a large fry pan. Sauté the onion, garlic and mushrooms until golden. Stir in the flour. Add remaining ingredients and simmer over moderate heat for 8 to 10 minutes, stirring occasionally. Heat another fry pan and add marinated steaks. Cover and cook for 5 to 7 minutes on each side. Add the sauce and simmer for a few minutes. Slice horizontally to serve.

Makes 4 servings.

Bistecca di Fegato di Vitello con Peperonata
Calf Liver Steak with Peppers

6 Slices of calf liver	6 oz. each	170 g each
Flour	2 tbsp.	30 ml
Olive oil	1/4 cup	60 ml
Sauce:		
Butter	1/4 cup	60 ml
Onion, sliced	1/2	1/2
Garlic clove, minced	1	1
Red pepper, sliced	1/2	1/2
Green pepper, sliced	1/2	1/2
Mushrooms, sliced	4	4
Tomato, chopped	1	1
Red or White wine	1/2 cup	120 ml
Oregano	1 pinch	1 pinch
Salt and pepper, to taste		

To make the sauce, heat butter in a large fry pan. Sauté onion, garlic and mushrooms for 5 minutes. Add remaining ingredients and cook for a few minutes, stirring occasionally. In another fry pan, heat oil. Dredge calf livers in flour and sauté for 4 minutes on each side. Add the sauce and simmer over moderate heat for 4 minutes.

Makes 6 servings.

Costolette di Vitello con Olive e Melanzana
Veal Chops with Olives and Eggplant

6 Veal chops	7 oz. each	200 g each
Marinade:		
Olive oil	3 tbsp.	50 ml
Garlic clove, minced	1	1
Dried sage	1 tsp.	5 ml
Crushed peppercorn	1 tsp.	5 ml
Sauce:		
Butter	3 tbsp.	50 ml
Green onions, chopped	4	4
Eggplant, peeled and diced	1	1
Flour	1 tbsp.	15 ml
Olives, chopped	1 cup	250 ml
Chicken broth (see recipe, p. 39)	1 cup	250 ml
35% cream	1 cup	250 ml
White wine	1/2 cup	120 ml
Salt and pepper, to taste		

Combine ingredients for the marinade. Add veal chops and marinate for 30 minutes. To make the sauce, heat butter in a fry pan and sauté green onions and eggplant until lightly browned. Stir in the flour. Add remaining ingredients and simmer over moderate heat for 8 minutes, stirring occasionally. Heat another large fry pan and add marinated veal chops. Cover and cook for 4 minutes on each side. Add the sauce and simmer over moderate heat for another 4 minutes.

Makes 6 servings.

Saltimbocca alla Romana
Veal Scallopini Roman Style

Saltimbocca translates as "leap into the mouth" which, no doubt, refers to its delicious taste.

8 Slices of veal, pounded	4 oz. each	115 g each
Prosciutto	8 slices	8 slices

Flour	3 tbsp.	50 ml
Butter	3 tbsp.	50 ml
Dried sage	1 tbsp.	15 ml

Sauce:

Olive oil	2 tbsp.	30 ml
Green onions, chopped	2	2
Flour	1 tbsp.	15 ml
Beef broth (see recipe, p. 42)	1 cup	250 ml
Marsala wine	1/2 cup	120 ml
Salt and pepper, to taste		

To make the sauce, heat oil in a fry pan and sauté green onions until lightly browned. Stir in flour. Add broth, wine, salt and pepper and simmer for 3 to 4 minutes. In another fry pan, heat butter. Top each slice of veal with one slice of prosciutto and dredge in flour. Sprinkle slices with sage and sauté for 2 minutes on each side. Add the sauce and simmer for a few minutes before serving.

Makes 8 servings.

Lamb

The best type of lamb to buy is "spring lamb." These animals have been milk-fed, producing meat that is mild in flavour and very tender. It used to be available only in spring, making it the traditional Easter dish. But you can now buy it frozen any time of the year. Just make sure you defrost it slowly in the refrigerator.

The best cuts of lamb are the leg and the rib chops. The latter can be cooked whole in a rack or sectioned. Two racks tied back to back in a circle makes an attractive crown roast.

When choosing a leg of lamb, the smaller it is, the more tender it will be. Between 4 to 7 pounds (2 to 3 kg) is about right.

Other cuts of lamb, such as shank and flank, are more tender and tasty if marinated overnight before cooking.

Some people prefer their lamb well done and other like it rare. I find rare difficult to digest, so my recipes will give you well-done meat that is still tender and juicy.

Costolette di Agnello al Vino Rosso
Lamb Chops with Red Wine Sauce

12 Lamb chops	3 oz. each	85 g each
Marinade:		
Olive oil	3 tbsp.	50 ml
Garlic cloves, smashed	2	2
Sugar	1 tbsp.	15 ml
Mint	2 tsp.	10 ml
Crushed peppercorn	1 tsp.	5 ml
Sauce:		
Butter	2 tbsp.	30 ml
Green onions, chopped	4	4
Flour	1 tbsp.	15 ml
Beef broth (see recipe, p. 42)	1 cup	250 ml
Red wine	1/2 cup	120 ml
Brandy or gin	2 tbsp.	30 ml
Juice of one orange		
Fresh parsley, chopped	1 tbsp.	15 ml
Salt and pepper, to taste		

Combine ingredients for the marinade. Add lamb chops and marinate for 30 minutes. To make the sauce, heat butter in a skillet and sauté the onion for 3 minutes. Stir in the flour. Add remaining ingredients and simmer over moderate heat for 6 minutes, stirring occasionally. Heat another fry pan and add the marinated lamb chops. Cover and sauté for 3 minutes on each side. Add the sauce and simmer briefly before serving.

Makes 4 to 6 servings.

Costolette di Agnello con Radica Forte e Crema
Lamb Chops with Horseradish and Cream Sauce

8 Lamb chops	3 oz. each	85 g each
Marinade:		
Olive oil	3 tbsp.	50 ml
Garlic cloves, chopped	2	2
Dried rosemary	1 tsp.	5 ml
Crushed peppercorn	1 tsp.	5 ml
Sauce:		
Butter	2 tbsp.	30 ml
Small onion, chopped	1	1
Green pepper, chopped	1/2	1/2
Flour	1 tbsp.	15 ml
Chicken broth	3/4 cup	180 ml
(see recipe, p. 39)		
White wine	1/2 cup	120 ml
35% cream	1/2 cup	120 ml
Prepared horseradish	1 tbsp.	15 ml
Salt and pepper, to taste		

Combine ingredients for the marinade. Add lamb chops and marinate for 30 minutes. To make the sauce, heat butter in a fry pan and sauté onion and green pepper until lightly browned. Stir in the flour. Add remaining ingredients and simmer over moderate heat for 8 minutes, stirring occasionally. Heat another fry pan and add marinated lamb chops. Cover and cook for 3 minutes on each side. Add the sauce and simmer an additional 5 minutes over moderate heat.

Makes 4 servings.

Stufato di Agnello
Lamb Casserole

Lamb meat, from the shoulder or leg, cubed	3 lbs.	1.4 kg
Vegetable oil	1/2 cup	120 ml
Onion, diced	1	1
Garlic cloves, minced	4	4
Mushrooms, sliced	2 cups	500 ml
Carrots, diced	3	3
Tomatoes, chopped	4	4
Red wine	1 cup	250 ml
Juice of 2 lemons		
Anchovy fillets	6	6
Bay leaves, crumbled	2	2
Dried mint	1 tbsp.	15 ml
Potatoes, peeled and diced	4	4
Tomato paste	1/4 cup	60 ml
Beef or other meat broth	1 quart	1 litre

In a large skillet or Dutch oven, heat oil and add lamb cubes. Cover and cook over moderate heat, stirring occasionally, for 10 to 15 minutes, or until browned. Add remaining ingredients, except potatoes, tomato paste and broth and simmer for 40 minutes, stirring frequently. Add the last three ingredients and simmer until the liquid reduces by half and the meat is tender.

Makes 4 to 6 servings.

Pork

Most of the pork consumed in Italy is salt-cured, or ground into sausages. Prosciutto, pancetta, mortadella, capocollo, and salami abound in Italian recipes.

If you are buying fresh pork, look for pale meat with firm, white fat. The darker the flesh, the older the animal and the tougher the meat. The best cuts are from the loin, especially the center part where you find the best roasts and the tenderloin. If you are making sausages, the best meat to use is from the shoulder or neck, which is lean and tasty.

One thing to remember is that pork should always be cooked thoroughly, without being dried out. These recipes will ensure that the meat stays tender and moist, even though it is well done.

Salsiccie di Carne
Fresh Pork Sausages

Pork shoulder	4 lbs.	2 kg
Salt	2 tbsp.	30 ml
Ground black pepper	2 tbsp.	30 ml
Small pork intestine	1	1 (about 10 ft./3 m long)

Using a manual or electric meat grinder, coarse-grind the meat. (If you don't have a meat grinder, ask your butcher to grind the meat for you.) Combine the ground meat with the salt and pepper in a large bowl. Work it with your hands until a piece of the mixture will stick to your hand when held upside-down. Remove the cutting blades from the grinder and attach the funnel piece. Slide one end of the intestine over the mouth of the funnel and work the entire length of it back over the attachment. With a string, tie off the end, which is left hanging. Push the pork mixture into the machine while rotating the handle until the meat begins to fill the casing. Ease the mixture into the casing with your free hand to ensure that the meat is firmly packed and there are no air bubbles. You may have to pin-prick the casing to release trapped air. When the casing is completely full, tie off the other end. Twist the sausage every 6 inches (15 cm) to create the individual links and tie these off with string. The sausages can be cooked fresh or air-dried for up to one week in a cantina. After that, you may store them in the freezer or packed in oil in jars. They will keep in oil for about 4 months.

Makes about fifteen 6-inch (15-cm) sausages.

Salsiccie Calabrese
Calabrian Sausage

Pork shoulder	4 lbs.	2 kg
Salt	2 tbsp.	30 ml
Ground black pepper	2 tbsp.	30 ml
Paprika	2 tbsp.	30 ml
Chili pepper	2 tbsp.	30 ml
Fennel seeds, chopped	1 tbsp.	15 ml
Small pork intestine	1	1

Coarsely grind the pork and mix thoroughly in a bowl with seasonings. Follow the above instructions for making basic sausage.

Salsiccie Abruzzese
Abruzzo-Style Sausage

Pork shoulder	4 lbs.	2 kg
Salt	2 tbsp.	30 ml
Ground black pepper	2 tbsp.	30 ml
Garlic cloves, minced	3	3
Peel of 2 oranges, minced		
Red wine	3/4 cup	180 ml

Finely grind the pork and mix thoroughly with remaining ingredients in a large bowl. Follow the above instructions for making basic sausage.

Tip: The pork must be ground finely in order to for the wine to be easily incorporated.

Salsiccie Piccante
Sausages with Hot Sauce

Fresh pork sausages	2 lbs.	900 g
Vegetable oil	2 tbsp.	30 ml
Chili pepper preserve (see recipe, p. 18)	1/4 cup	60 ml
Onion, chopped	1 cup	250 ml
Garlic cloves, minced	3	3

Tomato paste	1/4 cup	60 ml
Chicken or beef broth	1 cup	250 ml
(see recipes, p. 39/42)		
Red or white wine	1/2 cup	120 ml
Lemon juice	1/2 cup	120 ml
Wine vinegar	1/4 cup	60 ml
Sugar	2 tbsp.	30 ml
Salt and pepper, to taste		

In a large fry pan, combine sausages, oil and chili pepper preserve. Cover and simmer over medium heat for 8 minutes, turning sausages over occasionally. Add onion and garlic and continue cooking for 3 minutes. Add remaining ingredients, mixing well. Simmer for 20 minutes, stirring occasionally.

Makes 4 to 6 servings.

Salsiccie alla Cacciatore
Sausages Hunter Style

Fresh pork sausages	2 lbs.	900 g
Vegetable oil	2 tbsp.	30 ml
Aromatic preserve (see recipe, p. 17)	2 tbsp.	30 ml
Chili pepper preserve (see recipe, p. 18)	1 tbsp.	15 ml
Onion, thinly sliced	1	1
Red or green pepper, diced	1	1
Mushrooms, sliced	8	8
Garlic cloves, minced	2	2
Tomatoes, peeled	1 cup	250 ml
Chicken or beef broth	1 cup	250 ml
(see recipes, p. 39/42)		
Red wine	1/2 cup	120 ml
Salt and pepper, to taste		

In a large fry pan, combine sausages, oil and preserves. Cover and simmer over medium heat for 8 minutes, turning sausages over occasionally. Add onion, pepper, and mushrooms and continue cooking for 3 minutes. Add remaining ingredients and mix well. Simmer for 20 minutes, stirring occasionally until sauce is thick.

Makes 4 to 6 servings.

Costatine di Maiale con Miele e Vino
Spareribs with Honey and Wine Sauce

Pork back ribs, cut into sections of 4 ribs each	2 lbs.	900 g
Olive oil	1/4 cup	60 ml
Onion, chopped	1	1
Garlic cloves, minced	2	2
Chicken broth (see recipe, p. 39)	1/2 cup	120 ml
Red wine	1/2 cup	120 ml
Orange juice	1/2 cup	120 ml
Lemon juice	1/2 cup	120 ml
Honey	3 tbsp.	50 ml
Apple, peeled and chopped	1	1
Salt and pepper, to taste		

In a large fry pan, heat oil and add spareribs. Cover and sauté over high heat for 8 minutes on each side. Lower heat to medium and sauté onion and garlic until golden. Add remaining ingredients and simmer until spareribs are tender.

Makes 4 servings.

Scaloppine di Maiale con Pere e Brandy
Pork Scallopini with Pear and Brandy Sauce

12 Slices lean pork, pounded	3 oz. each	85 g each
Fine corn flour	1/4 cup	60 ml
Olive oil	1/3 cup	90 ml
Butter	2 tbsp.	30 ml
Beef broth (see recipe, p. 42)	1 cup	250 ml
Brandy	1/2 cup	120 ml
Pears, peeled and diced	2	2
Fresh lemon preserve (see recipe, p. 20)	2 tbsp.	30 ml
Chili pepper preserve (see recipe, p. 18)	1 tbsp.	15 ml
Salt and pepper, to taste		

In a large fry pan, heat oil and butter. Dredge each pork slice in corn flour and sauté for 2 minutes on each side. Lower heat to medium and add remaining ingredients. Cover and simmer for 5 minutes, stirring occasionally.

Makes 4 to 6 servings.

Filetto di Maiale con Salsa di Senape
Paillard of Pork Tenderloin with Mustard Sauce

2 Pork fillets, fat removed, butterflied and pounded	1 lb. each	450 g each
Olive oil	1/4 cup	60 ml
Shallots, chopped	1 cup	250 ml
Garlic cloves, minced	2	2
Chicken or beef broth (see recipes, p. 39/42)	1/2 cup	120 ml
Red wine	1/2 cup	120 ml
Lemon juice	1/2 cup	120 ml
10% cream, boiled	1/2 cup	120 ml
Tomatoes, chopped	1/2 cup	120 ml
Dry mustard	3 tbsp.	50 ml
Aromatic preserve (see recipe, p. 17)	2 tbsp.	30 ml
Salt and pepper, to taste		

In a large fry pan, heat oil and sauté pork fillets for 4 minutes on each side. Remove to a serving dish. Add shallots and garlic and sauté for 3 minutes. Add remaining ingredients and stir over moderate heat. Return fillets to pan, cover and simmer until the sauce reduces by half. Cut into slices to serve.

Makes 4 to 6 servings.

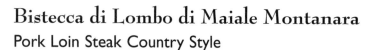

Bistecca di Lombo di Maiale Montanara
Pork Loin Steak Country Style

6 Pork loin steaks, butterflied and pounded	7 oz. each	200 g each

Marinade:

Dry mustard	2 tbsp.	30 ml
Olive oil	3 tbsp.	50 ml

Sauce:

Olive oil	3 tbsp.	50 ml
Green onions, chopped	4	4
Garlic cloves, minced	2	2
Bell peppers, sliced	1 cup	250 ml
Mushrooms, sliced	1 cup	250 ml
Asparagus tips	1 cup	250 ml
Beef stock (see recipe, p. 43)	1 cup	250 ml
White wine	1/2 cup	120 ml
Lemon juice	1/2 cup	120 ml
Aromatic preserve (see recipe, p. 17)	2 tbsp.	30 ml
Chili pepper preserve (see recipe, p. 18)	1 tbsp.	15 ml
Salt and pepper, to taste		

Combine ingredients for the marinade. Add pork and marinate for 15 to 30 minutes. To make the sauce, heat oil in a large fry pan and add all ingredients. Cover and simmer until vegetables are tender. Heat another fry pan and sauté marinated pork loins for 3 minutes on each side. Add the sauce and simmer briefly before serving.

Makes 6 servings.

Costolette di Maiale Impannate
Breaded Pork Chops

6 Pork loin chops	5 oz. each	140 g each
All-purpose flour	3 tbsp.	50 ml
Eggs, beaten	3	3
Milk	1/3 cup	90 ml
Breadcrumbs	2 cups	500 ml
Vegetable oil	3/4 cup	180 ml
Barbecue sauce	1 cup	250 ml

White wine	1/2 cup	120 ml
Aromatic preserve (see recipe, p. 17)	1/2 cup	120 ml
Rosemary, crushed	1 tbsp.	15 ml
Salt and pepper, to taste		

Place three bowls on the counter. In the first bowl, place flour; in the second, combine the beaten eggs and milk; and in the third, place the bread crumbs. One by one, dredge the pork chops in flour, dip them into the egg mixture, then dredge them in the breadcrumbs until well coated. In a large fry pan, heat oil and fry breaded pork chops for 5 minutes on each side, or until golden. Drain the oil and add remaining ingredients. Cover and simmer over low medium heat for 5 or 6 minutes, turning the chops occasionally.

Makes 6 servings.

Roasts

Arrosto di Manzo
Roast Beef

Beef standing rib roast	4 lbs.	1.8 kg
Marinade:		
Oil	1/4 cup	60 ml
Red wine or beer	1 cup	250 ml
Garlic cloves, chopped	2	2
Dry mustard	3 tbsp.	50 ml
Dried oregano	2 tbsp.	30 ml
Crushed peppercorn	1/4 cup	60 ml
Salt	1 tbsp.	15 ml
Beef broth or water	1 quart	1 litre

Preheat your oven to 500°F (260°C). Combine all ingredients for the marinade, except broth. Place beef in a large roasting pan and pour marinade over it, rubbing in the seasonings by hand. Place in oven and roast for 55 minutes. Lower the oven temperature to 400°F (205°C) and add the broth. Continue to cook for 1 hour, basting occasionally. When done, transfer the roast to a serving platter and keep warm. Skim the fat from the roasting juices. Strain the roasting liquid into a pot and bring to a boil. Carve your roast into thin slices and serve with the sauce.

Makes 6 servings.

Arrosto di Vitello
Roast Veal

Veal, top or bottom round	4 lbs.	1.8 kg

Marinade:

Vegetable oil	1/3 cup	90 ml
Lemon juice	1/2 cup	120 ml
White wine	1 cup	250 ml
Garlic cloves, chopped	6	6
Dried sage	2 tbsp.	30 ml
Salt and pepper, to taste		

Sauce:

Beef broth or water	1 quart	1 litre
Flour or cornstarch	2 tbsp.	30 ml
Red wine	1/2 cup	120 ml

Preheat your oven to 450°F (230°C). Combine ingredients for the marinade. Place the veal in a roasting pan and pour marinade over it, rubbing in the seasonings by hand. Place in oven and roast for 50 minutes. Lower heat to 375°F (190°C) and add the broth. Continue cooking for 1 hour, basting every 10 minutes. To check if roast is done, prick with a fork and if juices run clear, the meat is properly cooked. Transfer the roast to a serving platter and keep warm. Skim off the fat from the roasting juices. If there is not enough roasting liquid, deglaze the pan with some more broth. Strain into a pot and bring to a boil. Dissolve the flour in the wine and stir into the boiling broth, whisking well. Simmer over medium heat for 10 minutes, stirring occasionally. This makes about 3 cups (750 ml) of gravy. Carve your roast into thin slices and serve with gravy.

Serves 6 to 8 people.

Arrosto di Agnello
Roast Leg of Lamb

Boneless leg of lamb	4–5 lbs.	2 kg
Marinade:		
Vegetable oil	1/3 cup	90 ml
Red wine vinegar	1/2 cup	120 ml
Lemon juice	1/2 cup	120 ml
Onion, quartered	1	1
Garlic cloves, chopped	4	4
Celery stalks, chopped	2	2
Anchovy fillets	6	6
Dry mustard	2 tbsp.	30 ml
Dried rosemary	2 tbsp.	30 ml
Dried mint	2 tbsp.	30 ml
Salt and pepper, to taste		
Sauce:		
Beef or chicken broth (see recipes, p. 42/39)	1 quart	1 litre
Red wine	1 cup	250 ml
Tomato paste	2 tbsp.	30 ml
White wine	1/2 cup	120 ml
Cornstarch or flour	1/4 cup	60 ml

Preheat your oven to 475°F (245°C). Combine all ingredients for the marinade. Place the lamb in a roasting pan and pour the marinade over it, rubbing in the seasonings by hand. Place in oven, cover and cook for 55 minutes. Lower the oven temperature to 425°F (220°C). Combine the broth, red wine and tomato paste and add it to the roasting pan. Continue to cook for 40 minutes, basting occasionally. When done, transfer the roast to a serving platter and keep warm. Skim off the fat from the roasting juices. Strain the roasting liquid into a medium saucepan and bring to a boil. Dissolve the cornstarch in the white wine and stir into to the boiling broth. Simmer for 15 to 20 minutes until thickened. Carve your roast into slices and serve with some mint jelly, if desired.

Serves 6 to 8 people.

Arrosto di Maiale
Roast Pork

Pork loin roast, boneless	4 lbs.	1.8 kg
Marinade:		
Vegetable oil	1/3 cup	90 ml
Red wine vinegar	1/2 cup	120 ml
Apple juice	1/2 cup	120 ml
Liquid honey	1/2 cup	120 ml
Garlic cloves, chopped	8	8
Prepared mustard	2 tbsp.	30 ml
Dried rosemary	2 tbsp.	30 ml
Bay leaves, crumbled	2	2
Salt and pepper, to taste		
Sauce:		
Beef broth or water	1 quart	1 litre
Red wine	1 cup	250 ml
Orange juice	1 cup	250 ml
Potato flour	2 tbsp.	30 ml

Preheat your oven to 475°F (245°C). Combine all ingredients for the marinade. Place the pork loin in a roasting pan and pour the marinade over it, rubbing the seasonings in by hand. Place in oven and roast for 1 hour. Lower the oven temperature to 400°F (205°C) and add broth and wine. Continue to cook for another 55 minutes, basting occasionally. When done, transfer the roast to a serving platter and keep warm. Skim off as much fat as possible from the roasting juices. Strain the roasting liquid into a pot and bring to a boil. Dissolve the potato flour in the orange juice and whisk into the boiling broth. Simmer for 8 to 10 minutes, stirring occasionally until thickened.

Serves 6 to 8 people.

Egg Dishes

Eggs are very versatile. They can be used in a variety of dishes, in cakes, cookies and custards, in sauces and condiments, and in savoury dishes like quiche and omelets, or just eaten on their own.

While they do contain a lot of protein, they also contain cholesterol, which means we probably shouldn't eat them every day. But, once in a while, they're great.

The best eggs are fresh eggs, but most people don't have their own chickens, so here is one way to test for freshness. Hold the egg up to your ear and shake it. If you don't hear any sound, the egg is good and fresh. Another way is to place the egg in a bowl of water. If it sinks to the bottom, it is fresh. If it floats, it is stale and not good to use. The shell should be hard and free of cracks. Some people prefer brown eggs for baking because the yolks are a bit more yellow, but the colour of the shell does not affect the taste at all.

Uova Bollite
Boiled Eggs

Hard-boiled eggs can be eaten plain, devilled, or pickled, added to timballo, or made into egg salad.

Eggs	12	12
Water	3 quarts	3 litres
White vinegar	1/4 cup	60 ml
Salt	1 tbsp.	15 ml

Place the eggs in a large saucepan. Add salt and vinegar. Cover the eggs completely with water and bring to a gentle boil over medium heat. **For soft-boiled eggs:** let simmer for 3 minutes; for medium soft yolks, 5 minutes. **For hard-boiled eggs:** 10 minutes. Drop the eggs in cold water for a few seconds.

Serves 6.

Uova in Camicia
Poached Eggs

In Italy, we call poached eggs "uova in camicia," which means "eggs with a shirt." This is because they go into the water naked and come out with a little white coat on.

Eggs	12	12
Water	2 quarts	2 litres
White vinegar	1/4 cup	60 ml
Lemon juice	1/4 cup	60 ml
Salt	1 tsp.	5 ml

In a large skillet, combine water, lemon juice, vinegar and salt. Bring to a gentle boil over medium heat. Break the eggs into cups, one by one, and slide into simmering water. Boil for 3 to 4 minutes, more if you prefer them hard-boiled. Remove eggs with a slotted spoon, and drop into ice water to stop the cooking process. Remove eggs from cold water, allowing excess water to drip off.

Serves 6.

Uova a Occhio di Bue
Fried Eggs

For an old-fashioned brunch, serve with buttered toast, home fried potatoes and crispy bacon.

Eggs	12	12
Clarified butter or vegetable oil	3/4 cup	180 ml
Salt	1 tbsp.	15 ml

In a heavy skillet, heat clarified butter. Break the eggs into a bowl, making sure they are free of any bits of shell. Slide 6 eggs at a time into skillet and reduce heat to medium. Fry for about 3 minutes or until the whites are firm. For "sunny-side up", baste top of eggs with pan butter as they cook. For "over-easy", turn eggs over with a slotted spatula when almost done and fry for another 30 seconds.

Serves 6.

Uova Strapazzate
Scrambled Eggs

If you are preparing brunch, serve this with toast and homemade jam, hash browns, and fruit salad.

Eggs	12	12
Cream or milk	1/2 cup	120 ml
Butter	1/4 cup	60 ml
Vegetable oil	2 tbsp.	30 ml
Salt	1 tsp.	5 ml

Break the eggs into a bowl and add salt and milk. Whip them well. Heat butter and oil in a skillet over medium heat. Add the beaten eggs and stir them with a wooden spoon until light and fluffy.

Serves 6.

Omeletta di Vegetali
Vegetable Omelet

A number of fresh ingredients can be added to your omelet. Try fresh herbs, chopped tomato, grated cheese, diced ham or smoked salmon. The choices are endless.

Eggs	4	4
Salt and pepper, to taste		
Vegetable oil	1/4 cup	60 ml
Butter	2 tbsp.	30 ml
Mushrooms, sliced	1/2 cup	120 ml
Green onions, chopped	1	1
OR half a small white onion		
Red peppers, sliced	1/2 cup	120 ml
Black olives, chopped	1/4 cup	60 ml

Beat eggs well and season with salt and pepper. In an omelet pan, heat oil and butter. Sauté mushrooms, onions and peppers over medium heat for 3 to 4 minutes, or until soft. Pour in eggs, add olives, and let cook for 2 minutes. When firm, flip the egg mixture over with a spatula and cook for another minute. Cut the omelet in half and keep warm.

Serves 2.

Frittata con Asparagi
Frittata with Asparagus

Vegetable oil	1/2 cup	120 ml
Butter	3 tbsp.	50 ml
Fresh asparagus	1 bunch	1 bunch
Green onion, chopped	2	2
Eggs	12	12
Milk	1/2 cup	120 ml
All-purpose flour	1/4	60 ml
Provolone cheese, shredded	1 cup	250 ml
Parmesan cheese	1/4 cup	60 ml
Salt and pepper, to taste		

In a large fry pan, heat oil and butter. Sauté asparagus and green onion for 3 to 5 minutes, or until tender. In a bowl, beat eggs with remaining ingredients and pour into fry pan, stirring gently. Reduce heat and cook until eggs are nearly set. Carefully flip the frittata over and continue to cook over medium low heat until golden brown.

Serves 4 to 6.

Frittata con Bocconcini e Salsiccie
Frittata with Bocconcini and Sausages

Vegetable oil	3/4 cup	180 ml
Eggs	8	8
10% cream or milk	1 cup	250 ml
All-purpose flour	1 cup	250 ml
Green onions or white cooking onions, chopped	1 cup	250 ml
Italian sausages, thinly sliced	2 cups	500 ml
Bocconcini, shredded	8	8
OR Mozzarella, shredded	about 2 cups	500 ml
Parmesan cheese, grated	1/2 cup	120 ml
Salt and pepper, to taste		

Heat oil in a large fry pan. In a large bowl, beat eggs with remaining ingredients. Pour into fry pan, stirring gently. Cook until eggs are almost set. Remove from heat and place fry pan in preheated 375°F (190°C) oven for 20 minutes, or until frittata is golden brown on top. Turn out onto a serving dish and cut into wedges.

Serves 4.

Frittata di Ricotta
Ricotta Frittata

Vegetable or olive oil	3/4 cup	180 ml
Large eggs	8	8
Ricotta cheese	1 lb.	450 g
Milk or 10% cream	1 cup	250 ml
All-purpose flour	1 cup	250 ml
Parmesan cheese, grated	1/2 cup	120 ml
Parsley, chopped	1/2 cup	120 ml
Salt and pepper, to taste		

In a large fry pan, heat the oil over moderate heat. In a large bowl, whisk together remaining ingredients until smooth. Pour into fry pan and stir gently with a wooden spoon. When the frittata has browned on one side, drain the oil and invert the frittata onto a plate. Flip it back, moist side down, into the fry pan with the oil and cook until browned. It should take 10 to 15 minutes for each side. Cut into wedges and serve.

Makes 4 to 6 servings.

Screpelle
Crêpes

This recipe can be used for making both savoury and dessert crêpes.

Eggs	3	3
Milk or cold water	3 cups	750 ml
All-purpose flour	3 cups	750 ml
Salt	1 tsp.	5 ml
Vegetable oil	as needed	as needed

Break the eggs into a stainless steel bowl, making sure no bits of shell get in. Add milk and whisk for 2 to 3 minutes. Add flour and salt and continue whisking until all lumps are gone and mixture is smooth. Let the batter rest in the refrigerator for 30 minutes. Heat a non-stick crêpe pan over medium heat; brush with 1/2 tsp. (2.5 ml) of oil. Ladle about 1/4 cup (60 ml) of batter into pan and tilt the pan so that batter coats bottom. Cook for 30 seconds on each side or until light and golden. Slide the crêpe onto a plate and repeat the procedure with remaining batter. To serve the crêpes, fill them with your choice of filling and roll them or fold them into quarters.

Makes 18 crêpes.

Rotolino di Ricotta e Spinaci
Ricotta and Spinach Roulade

Crêpes (see recipe above)	6	6
Tomato sauce (see recipe, p. 27)	1 quart	1 litre
Béchamel sauce (see recipe, p. 24)	2 cups	500 ml
Filling:		
Ricotta cheese	2 lbs.	900 g
Frozen spinach, thawed, strained and chopped	1 lb.	450 g
Eggs	4	4
Bread crumbs	1 cup	250 ml
Parmesan cheese, grated	1 cup	250 ml
Parsley, chopped	1/2 cup	120 ml
Nutmeg, grated	1 tsp.	5 ml
Salt and pepper	1 tbsp. mixed	15 ml mixed

Preheat your oven to 375°F (190°C). To make filling, combine all ingredients in a large bowl and knead by hand for 3 to 5 minutes. Spread the filling evenly onto the crêpes with a spatula and roll each crêpe. Pour the tomato sauce into a medium-sized baking dish. Arrange the roulades in the dish and cover with the béchamel sauce. Bake for 35 to 45 minutes or until bubbling. Turn off the heat and let the roulades sit in the oven for another 10 minutes before serving.

Makes 3 large or 6 small servings.

Vegetable Side Dishes and Entrées

In an Italian meal, the vegetables or *contorni* can be eaten at the same time as the main course, but are always served on a separate dish from the meat or fish. They can even form the main course in a light lunch or supper.

Buy your vegetables fresh whenever you can. Look for produce that is firm, crisp and unblemished. Use them as soon as possible after buying, or else store them in the refrigerator, except for gourds, onions, garlic and potatoes, which can be stored in a cool, dark place. In some recipes, frozen or canned vegetables can be substituted for fresh ones.

Try not to overcook your vegetables, as they lose most of their nutritious value when cooked for too long. I prefer mine al dente, tender but still with some bite. If you are boiling them, make sure the water is at a full boil before you add them. This will reduce the loss of vitamins and preserve the colour.

Melanzana in Padella alla Parmigiana
Pan-Cooked Eggplant Parmigiana

Medium eggplant	1	1
Lemon juice	1/4 cup	60 ml
Salt	1 tbsp.	15 ml
Vegetable oil	1/2 cup	120 ml
All-purpose flour	1 cup	250 ml
Tomato sauce (see recipe, p. 27)	2 cups	500 ml
Mozzarella cheese, sliced	8 oz.	225 g

Peel and slice the eggplant into 1/2-inch (1-cm) thick rounds. Place the slices in a bowl with the salt and lemon juice and let them sit for two hours, mixing occasionally. Drain and wash the eggplant well. In a large fry pan, heat the oil. Coat each eggplant slice in the flour and fry in the oil until golden on both sides. Continue frying until all the eggplant is used up. When you are done frying, remove any excess oil from the pan. Cover the bottom of the fry pan with the fried eggplant slices and top each one with a tablespoon of tomato sauce and one slice of mozzarella. Layer the tomato sauce and cheese two more times on top of each slice, making sure to end with a layer of cheese. Cover the pan and return it to the burner. Cook over low heat just until the cheese melts.

Makes 4 to 6 servings.

Broccoli Affogati
Braised Broccoli

This method of cooking may also be used for cauliflower, carrots, or asparagus. Peeling broccoli and asparagus stems removes the tough skin.

Broccoli, peeled	2 bunches	2 bunches
Vegetable oil	1/4 cup	60 ml
Chicken broth (see recipe, p. 39)	1 cup	250 ml
Onion, minced	1	1
Garlic cloves, minced	2	2
Red pepper, seeded and julienned	1	1
Salt and pepper, to taste		

Combine all ingredients in a large skillet. Cover and steam-sauté for 6 to 8 minutes or until broccoli is tender. Adjust seasoning, if necessary.

Serves 4.

Rapini Affogati
Braised Broccoli Rabe

This dish also tastes great as a cold leftover sandwich.

Olive oil	3/4 cup	180 ml
Garlic cloves, minced	4	4
Onion, finely sliced	1	1
Rapini, peeled	2 bunches	2 bunches
Chicken broth or water	1 cup	250 ml
Crushed peppercorn	1 tbsp.	15 ml
Salt, to taste		

In a large fry pan, heat oil and sauté garlic and onion for 2 minutes, until transparent. Add rapini, broth, pepper, and salt and cover. Simmer over medium heat, stirring occasionally, until liquid is absorbed.

Serves 4.

Patate Stufate in Padella
Stewed Potatoes

This dish makes a nice accompaniment to roasts and meat dishes.

Potatoes, peeled and quartered	3 lbs.	1.4 kg
Vegetable oil	1/2 cup	120 ml
Onion, sliced	1	1
Garlic clove, minced	1	1
Tomatoes, chopped	1 cup	250 ml
Chicken or vegetable stock	2 cups	500 ml
(see recipes, p. 40/42)		
Red or green pepper, sliced	1	1
Dried basil	1 tbsp.	30 ml
Salt and pepper, to taste		
Fresh parsley, chopped	1 tbsp.	15 ml

Combine all ingredients except parsley in a large fry pan and bring to a boil. Cover and lower heat to medium. Simmer, stirring occasionally, until potatoes are tender. Transfer to a serving dish and garnish with chopped parsley.

Serves 4 to 6.

Patate Ripiene
Stuffed Potatoes

Potatoes (about 6 medium)	3 lbs.	1.3 kg
Sour cream	1 cup	250 ml
Bread crumbs	1/2 cup	120 ml
Parmesan cheese, grated	1/2 cup	120 ml
Green onion, chopped	1/2 cup	120 ml
Cooked ham, chopped	1/2 cup	120 ml
Eggs	3	3
Salt and pepper, to taste		

Pierce the potatoes with a fork. Bake in a 425°F (220°C) oven for about 1 hour, until tender and cooked through. Cool slightly. Remove the tops of the potatoes by slicing them lengthwise. Scoop out the pulp with a spoon and mash while still warm. Add remaining ingredients to mashed potatoes and mix well. Spoon mixture evenly into potato shells and return to 375°F (190°C) oven for 20 minutes, or until golden on top.

Serves 6.

Giardiniera di Vegetali in Padella
Garden-Style Braised Vegetables

You can serve this as an entrée or side dish.

Carrots, peeled and sliced	4	4
Potatoes, peeled and sliced	2	2
Zucchini, sliced	2	2
Broccoli, chopped	1 head	1 head
Mushrooms, sliced in half	6	6
Fennel bulb, chopped	1	1
Belgian endive, quartered	1 head	1 head
Vegetable stock or chicken broth	1 cup	250 ml
(see recipes, p. 42/39)		
Vegetable oil	1/4 cup	60 ml
Fresh onion preserve (see recipe, p. 20)	1/4 cup	60 ml
Aromatic preserve (see recipe, p. 17)	2 tbsp.	30 ml
Salt and pepper, to taste		

In a large fry pan or skillet, arrange all the chopped vegetables. Add the remaining ingredients and cover skillet. Steam-sauté over moderate heat for 8 to 10 minutes, or until vegetables are tender.

Makes 4 servings.

Funghi Ripiene con Pancetta
Stuffed Mushroom Caps with Pancetta

This recipe can be served as a side dish or as a savoury appetizer.

Large mushrooms	12	12
Bread crumbs	1 cup	250 ml
Pancetta, finely chopped	1 cup	250 ml
Eggs	3	3
Parmesan cheese, grated	1/4 cup	60 ml
Parsley, chopped	1/2 cup	120 ml
Garlic cloves, minced	3	3
Fresh basil, chopped	2 tbsp.	30 ml
(or basil condiment, see recipe p. 18)		

Chicken allows all cooks to use their creativity as it goes well with so many ingredients. Shown here is Chicken Breasts with Olives (page 105).

A honey-based marinade contrasts deliciously with the savoury flavour of roast pork (page 140).

Beef Stew is a hearty and satisfying meal for those chilly winter evenings (page 118).

Vegetable Omelet (page 143). Many believe that an omelet is cooked in a pan, while a fritatta is baked, but it really doesn't matter how you cook it.

Pan-Cooked Eggplant Parmigiana (page 149).

Garden Salad (page 159)
can be served after the main
course or as an appetizer.

Salt and pepper, to taste		
Vegetable oil	1/3 cup	90 ml

Clean the mushrooms and remove the stems. Finely chop stems and combine with remaining ingredients except the oil. Mix well for 3 to 5 minutes. Divide the stuffing evenly between the mushroom caps. In a large skillet or fry pan, heat the oil over moderate heat. Add the stuffed mushroom caps and cook for 15 to 20 minutes, covered, until firm and golden on top.

Makes 4 to 6 servings.

Peperoni Ripiene in Padella
Stuffed Pepper Casserole

The minced beef in this recipe may be replaced with veal, pork, or chicken.

Green peppers, cored	6	6
Vegetable oil	1/2 cup	120 ml
Tomatoes, peeled and chopped	1 cup	250 ml
Chicken broth (see recipe, p. 39)	1 1/2 cup	375 ml
Stuffing:		
Minced beef	2 lbs.	900 g
Bread crumbs	1 cup	250 ml
Onion, chopped	2 tbsp.	30 ml
Garlic cloves, minced	2	2
Parsley, chopped	1/2 cup	120 ml
Parmesan cheese, grated	1/2 cup	120 ml
Eggs	4	4
All-purpose flour	1/4 cup	60 ml
Salt and pepper, to taste		

For stuffing, combine all ingredients in a bowl and mix well until incorporated. Spoon stuffing into peppers, pressing it well in. In a large skillet, heat oil and sauté stuffed peppers until brown on each side. Add tomatoes and broth and lower heat to medium. Cover skillet and let peppers simmer for 40 minutes, turning occasionally. You may have to add additional broth if liquid evaporates.

Serves 6.

Cappuci Ripiene in Padella

Cabbage Roll Casserole

Savoy cabbage	1	1
Canned tomatoes, chopped	2 cups	500 ml
Fresh tomatoes, chopped	2	2
Chicken broth (see recipe, p. 39)	1 cup	250 ml

Stuffing:

Ground meat (pork, veal, and/or beef)	1 1/2 lbs.	675 g
Boiled rice	2 cups	500 ml
Pancetta, chopped	1 cup	250 ml
Bread crumbs	1/2 cup	120 ml
Eggs	4	4
Green onion, chopped	4	4
Garlic cloves, minced	2	2
All-purpose flour	2 tbsp.	30 ml
Parsley, chopped	1/2 cup	120 ml
Paprika	2 tbsp.	30 ml
Salt and pepper, to taste		

Bring a large pot of salted water to a boil over medium heat. Blanch cabbage for 6 to 8 minutes. Run under cold water and separate leaves. For the stuffing, mix all ingredients in a bowl until well incorporated. Spoon stuffing into the center of each cabbage leaf and roll up. Place cabbage rolls in a large saucepan with canned tomatoes, fresh tomatoes, and broth and bring to a simmer over medium heat. Cook for 40 to 55 minutes. You may have to add more broth while cooking if the liquid evaporates.

Serves 4 to 6.

Salads and Dressings

In Italy, the salad is served after the main course and before the cheese to cleanse the mouth and refresh the palate.

Everything in your salad should be as fresh as possible, especially the lettuce. The leaves should be crisp, not wilted, and they should always be torn by hand, never cut with a knife as this bruises the leaves.

A salad which is comprised of lettuce, or various greens is called *insalata verde* (green salad). A salad which has other vegetables and ingredients mixed in is called *insalata mista* (mixed salad). These other ingredients can be foods like cooked turkey or chicken, tuna or salmon, cured meats, pasta, beans, and rice, to name a few. A good, hearty salad can really be a meal unto itself.

Whatever your preference, one of the most important ingredients is the dressing which should complement the salad, without overpowering it.

Condimento alla Cesare
Caesar Dressing

Egg yolks	8	8
Garlic cloves, minced	6	6
Anchovy fillets	12	12
Capers	1/2 cup	120 ml
Prepared mustard	4 tbsp.	60 ml
Lemon juice	1/2 cup	120 ml
Hot pepper sauce	1 tbsp.	15 ml
Olive or vegetable oil	3 cups	750 ml
Red wine vinegar	1/3 cup	90 ml
Salt and pepper to taste		

Combine all ingredients except oil and vinegar in stainless steel bowl. Whisk until eggs thicken. Slowly add half the oil in a thin stream and continue whisking until thick and creamy. In a small pot, bring vinegar to a boil. Slowly add to the egg mixture, whisking constantly. Continue to add in the remaining oil in a thin stream while whisking. The heat from the vinegar will slightly cook the egg yolks, which will allow you to store this dressing for a longer period of time. Serve immediately with Parmesan cheese and croutons, or refrigerate for up to 3 weeks.

Makes about 4 cups/1 litre.

Olio e Aceto
Italian Dressing

This makes a nice, light dressing for tossed or marinated salads.

Olive oil	2 cups	500 ml
Red wine vinegar	1 cup	250 ml
Lemon juice	1/2 cup	120 ml
Dry mustard	1 tbsp.	15 ml
Garlic cloves, minced	2	2
Dried oregano	1 tbsp.	15 ml
Sugar	2 tbsp.	30 ml

In a stainless steel bowl, whisk all ingredients together until incorporated. Serve immediately or refrigerate.

Makes about 4 cups/1 litre.

Condimento alla Prima Donna
Prima Donna Dressing

Mayonnaise (see recipe, p. 25)	1 cup	250 ml
Chili pepper preserve (see recipe, p. 18)	1 cup	250 ml
Lemon juice	1/2 cup	120 ml
Sour cream	1/2 cup	120 ml
Stuffed olives, chopped	1 cup	250 ml
Capers, finely chopped	1/4 cup	60 ml
Dill pickles, finely chopped	2	2
Hard-boiled eggs, diced	4	4
Hot pepper sauce	1 tsp.	5 ml
OR Chili pepper preserve	1 tbsp.	15 ml
(see recipe, p. 18)		
Sugar	2 tbsp.	30 ml
Salt and pepper, to taste		

Place all ingredients in a stainless steel bowl and whisk together for 2 to 4 minutes, or process in a food processor for a smoother consistency.

This dressing may be kept in the refrigerator in a tightly covered container for up to one month.

Makes about 6 cups/1 1/2 litres.

Condimento Gorgonzola
Gorgonzola Dressing

White vinegar	1/2 cup	120 ml
Lemon juice	1/4 cup	60 ml
Water	3/4 cup	180 ml
Gorgonzola cheese	10 oz.	285 g
Mayonnaise (see recipe p. 25)	1 cup	250 ml
Sour cream	3/4 cup	180 ml
Celery salt	1/4 cup	60 ml
Salt and pepper, to taste		

In a small pot, bring the vinegar, lemon juice and water to a boil. Place the cheese in a large bowl and pour the boiling vinegar mixture over the cheese to soften it. Mix together to form a soft consistency. Let the mixture cool for about 30 minutes before adding the remaining ingredients. Whisk together until smooth and creamy.

This dressing may be stored in tightly covered jars in the refrigerator for 2 to 3 weeks.

Makes about 3 cups/750 ml.

Condimento alla Francese
French Dressing

Tomato paste	2 tbsp.	30 ml
White vinegar	1/2 cup	120 ml
Red wine vinegar	1/4 cup	60 ml
Lemon juice	1/2 cup	120 ml
Ketchup	1 cup	250 ml
Mayonnaise (see recipe, p. 25)	2 cups	500 ml
Sugar	2 tbsp.	30 ml
Paprika	1 tbsp.	15 ml
Salt and pepper, to taste		

In a large bowl, dilute the tomato paste with the vinegar and lemon juice, mixing well. Add remaining ingredients and whisk vigorously until the dressing is creamy and pink in colour.

This dressing may be preserved in tightly covered jars in the refrigerator for up to two weeks.

Makes about 4 cups/1 litre.

Insalata Caprese
Tomato and Bocconcini Salad

Caprese salad is so called because it is made in the style of Capri.

Romaine or iceberg lettuce	4 leaves	4 leaves
Tomatoes, sliced into rounds	4	4
Fresh bocconcini, sliced	6	6
Olive oil	3/4 cup	180 ml
Wine vinegar	1/2 cup	120 ml
Anchovy fillets, chopped	6	6
Fresh basil leaves, minced	4	4
Salt and pepper		
Cucumber, sliced (optional)		

Arrange lettuce leaves on a serving dish and top with slices of tomato. On each tomato slice, place one round slice of bocconcini. Whisk together the oil, vinegar, anchovies, basil, salt and pepper and pour over the salad. Serve immediately, garnished with some sliced cucumber, if desired.

Serves 4.

Insalata Cesare
Caesar Salad

Head of romaine lettuce	1	1
Caesar dressing (see recipe, p. 155)	1 cup	250 ml
Parmesan cheese	1 cup	250 ml
Croutons (see recipe below)	2 cups	500 ml

Tear romaine lettuce into bite-size pieces. In a large bowl, combine lettuce with dressing, cheese and croutons. Toss well and serve immediately.

Serves 4 to 6.

Crostini

Croutons

This is a great recipe for using up stale bread.

Italian or French bread, cubed	8 slices	8 slices
Vegetable oil	3 tbsp.	50 ml
Parmesan cheese, grated	1/2 cup	120 ml
Salt and pepper, to taste		

Preheat your oven to 325°F (160°C). Combine all ingredients in a baking dish, making sure that bread cubes are well coated. Roast them in the oven, stirring them occasionally, until they are dry and golden brown. Let them cool. Use immediately or store in a covered container for future use.

Makes about 4 cups/1 litre.

Insalata Ortolana

Garden Salad

This salad also makes an appealing appetizer.

Fennel bulb, cut into wedges	1	1
Head of radicchio, cut into wedges	1	1
Head of celery, cut into wedges	1	1
Green or red pepper, Cored and julienned	1	1
Carrots, peeled and quartered	2	2
Dressing:		
Tomato, seeded and chopped	1	1
Olive or vegetable oil	1/2 cup	120 ml
Lemon juice	1/2 cup	120 ml
Balsamic or red wine vinegar	1/3 cup	90 ml
Dry mustard	2 tbsp.	30 ml
Dried oregano	1 tsp.	15 ml
Crushed peppercorn	1 tbsp.	15 ml

Arrange vegetables on a large serving platter. For the dressing, combine all ingredients in a blender or food processor and blend for about 2 minutes, or you can whisk it by hand if you have the energy. Pour the dressing over the vegetables and store any leftover in the refrigerator.

Serves 4.

Insalata di Avocado con Indivia
Endive and Avocado Salad

Avocado pears, pitted,	2	2
Belgian endive, quartered	4	4
Red onion, sliced	1	1
Small cucumber, sliced	1	1
Tomato, sliced	1	1

Dressing:

Olive oil	3/4 cup	180 ml
Lemon juice	1/2 cup	120 ml
Balsamic vinegar	1/4 cup	60 ml
Liquid honey	1 tbsp.	15 ml
Green onion, chopped	1/2 cup	120 ml
Prepared mustard	2 tbsp.	30 ml
Dried oregano	1 tsp.	5 ml
Salt and pepper		

Arrange the vegetables on a large serving platter. for the dressing, combine all ingredients in a jar and seal tight. Shake well and pour over vegetables.

Serves 4.

Insalata Misto con Condimento di Aceto Balsamico
Chef's Salad with Balsamic Vinaigrette

Mixed salad greens	4 handfuls	4 handfuls
Radicchio	1 handful	1 handful
Tomatoes, sliced	2	2
Cucumber, peeled and sliced	1	1

Dressing:

Olive oil	1/2 cup	120 ml
Balsamic vinegar	1/2 cup	120 ml
Lemon juice	1/4 cup	60 ml
Sugar	1 tbsp.	15 ml
Dry mustard	1 tbsp.	15 ml
Dried oregano	1 tbsp.	15 ml
Salt and pepper, to taste		

To make the dressing, combine all the ingredients in a jar or squeeze bottle and shake well. Store in the refrigerator until ready to use. To serve, place the greens, radicchio, tomatoes and cucumber in a bowl and toss well with the dressing.

Makes 4 to 6 servings.

Insalata di Cappuci Agrodolce
Sweet and Sour Cabbage

Medium cabbage, shredded	1	1
Green or red peppers, Seeded and sliced	2	2
Medium onion, sliced	1	1
Vegetable oil	3/4 cup	180 ml
White vinegar	1/2 cup	120 ml
Lemon juice	1/4 cup	60 ml
Sugar	1/4 cup	60 ml
Salt and pepper		
Tomato, quartered, for garnish	2	2

In a stainless steel bowl, combine all ingredients and toss thoroughly for about 3 minutes. Serve on a plate and garnish with tomato slices.

Note: This salad will keep for about a week in the refrigerator, and actually tastes better on the second day, although you may have to drain it.

Serves 4.

Fagiolini Insalata
Green Bean Salad

This salad goes well on a picnic with some garlic bread and cold cuts.

Green beans, ends cut off	2 lbs.	900 g
Olive oil	3/4 cup	180 ml
White vinegar	1/2 cup	120 ml
Red onion, finely sliced	1	1
Garlic cloves, minced	3	3
Fresh mint leaves, julienned	10	10
Dried mint	2 tbsp.	30 ml
Dried basil	1 tsp.	5 ml
Salt and pepper		
Tomato, quartered, for garnish	2	2

Bring a pot of salted water to a boil. Add green beans and boil until tender, about 15 to 20 minutes. Drain and rinse under cold water. Combine beans and remaining ingredients in a large bowl and toss thoroughly. Garnish with tomato slices, if desired.

Serves 4.

Insalata di Frutta Fresca
Fresh Fruit Salad

This is a great recipe to use up all that overripe fruit in the refrigerator.

Apples, peeled and diced	2	2
Oranges, sectioned	2	2
Pears, peeled and diced	2	2
Cantaloupe or Honey dew melon, diced	1/2	1/2
Seedless grapes	2 cups	500 ml
Strawberries, hulled and sliced	1 pint	500 ml
Orange juice	1/2 cup	120 ml
Lemon juice	1/2 cup	120 ml
Sugar	1/4 cup	60 ml

Toss all ingredients together in a bowl. Serve as is or with a dollop of whipped cream and some chopped walnuts or pecans.

Serves 4 to 6.

Insalata Mista con Salmone
Tossed Salad with Salmon

If you don't like salmon, this salad can also be made with tuna fish, or even shrimps, crab or lobster meat.

Iceberg lettuce	1 head	1 head
Canned pink salmon	7 oz.	213 g
Walnuts or pecans	1 cup	250 ml
Red pepper, cored and diced	1	1
Green onions, chopped	4	4
Avocado, peeled and diced	1	1
Tomatoes, wedged (for garnish)	4	4

Dressing:

Olive oil	3/4 cup	180 ml
Lemon juice	1/2 cup	120 ml
Balsamic vinegar	1/4 cup	60 ml
White vinegar	1/4 cup	60 ml
Prepared mustard	2 tbsp.	30 ml
Garlic cloves, minced	2	2
Salt and pepper, to taste		

To make the dressing, whisk all ingredients together in a large bowl until creamy. Break lettuce into bite-sized pieces and add to the dressing along with remaining ingredients. Toss together until well coated and garnish with tomato slices.

Makes 4 to 6 servings.

Insalata di Riso con Curry e Gamberetti
Rice Salad with Curry and Baby Shrimp

Arborio or long-grain rice	1 cup	250 ml
Baby shrimp, cooked and peeled	2 cups	500 ml
Red pepper, diced	1 cup	250 ml
Apples, peeled, cored, and diced	2	2
Celery stalks, chopped	2	2
Olive oil	3/4 cup	180 ml
Lemon juice	1/2 cup	120 ml
White vinegar	1/3 cup	90 ml
Sour cream or mayonnaise	1/2 cup	120 ml
Curry powder	2 tbsp.	30 ml
Salt and pepper		
Hard-boiled eggs (for garnish)	4	4

Bring a pot of salted water to a rolling boil. Add rice and reduce heat to simmer. Cook rice until tender.

Tip: Arborio rice will take about 18 minutes to cook. Long-grain rice will take about 30 minutes.

Drain and rinse under cold water. In a large bowl, toss rice with remaining ingredients until well coated. Transfer to a serving platter and garnish with wedges of boiled egg, if desired.

Serves 4.

Insalata di Patate con Uova Sode
Potato Salad with Boiled Eggs

Medium potatoes	3 lbs.	1.4 kg
Eggs, hard boiled, chopped	4	4
Green onion, chopped	4	4
Red pepper, cored and diced	1	1
Mayonnaise (see recipe, p. 25)	1 cup	250 ml
Olive oil	1/3 cup	90 ml
White vinegar	1/4 cup	60 ml
Salt and pepper		
Sliced tomato and cucumber for garnish		

Place the potatoes in a pot. Cover with cold, salted water and bring to a simmer. Cook until potatoes are fork tender. Drain, run under cold water, and dice. In a large bowl, combine potatoes with remaining ingredients and toss gently until well coated. Garnish with sliced tomato and cucumber, if desired.

Serves 4.

Insalata di Radicchio e Affettati
Radicchio Salad with Cold Cuts

Any type of mild cheese like provolone or friulano works well in this salad.

Heads of radicchio, julienned	2	2
Red onion, finely sliced	1	1
Prosciutto, julienned	4 slices	4 slices
Cooked ham, julienned	4 slices	4 slices
Smoked turkey, julienned	4 slices	4 slices
Cheese, sliced	2/3 cup	150 ml
Cucumber, sliced (for garnish)	1	1
Dressing:		
Olive or vegetable oil	3/4 cup	180 ml
Lemon juice	1/2 cup	120 ml
Wine vinegar	1/2 cup	120 ml
Dry mustard	1 tbsp.	15 ml
Dried oregano	1 tbsp.	15 ml
Crushed peppercorn	1 tbsp.	15 ml
Salt	1 tsp.	5 ml

To make dressing, whisk all ingredients together until smooth. Combine all ingredients, except cucumber, in a large bowl and add dressing. Toss together until well coated. Serve on a large platter, garnished with cucumber slices.

Makes 4 to 6 servings.

Dessert

The end to an Italian meal is usually signaled by a selection of fine cheese and fresh fruit, or a sweet, simple dessert followed by espresso and a fine liqueur. Please see the list of cheese on page 10 to get an idea of the variety that is available.

If you only have room for the liqueur, here are a few popular Italian spirits that make a nice *digestivo* and a fine accompaniment to a *demitasse* of espresso.

Amaretto

A sweet, almond flavoured liqueur.

Frangelica

A sweet blend of roasted hazelnuts and 34 selected herbs and berries.

Grappa

A distilled spirit made from pressed grape skins.

Marsala

This is a fortified wine but it makes a lovely after-dinner drink. The *cremovo* is like a sweet cream sherry and is reminiscent of almonds or cherries. Makes an excellent sipping wine.

Sambuca

A clear, licorice flavoured liqueur, also known as *anisetta*. Traditionally served flamed *con le mosche* (with flies) with whole coffee beans floating in the glass.

Strega

A sweet, yellow licorice and citrus flavoured liqueur made from over 70 herbs.

Vecchia Romagna

This brandy is aged in oak for more than 10 years to create a smooth taste.

Salsa di Cioccolata
Chocolate Sauce

Chocolate chips	10 oz.	285 g
Vegetable oil	2 tbsp.	30 ml
Brown sugar	1/2 cup	120 ml
Coffee or water	1/2 cup	120 ml

Combine the chocolate and oil in a stainless steel bowl. Place the bowl over a pot with gently simmering water, making sure that no moisture comes in contact with the chocolate. Melt chocolate, stirring occasionally. When melted, add in the sugar and coffee and whisk until the mixture comes to a boil. Cool slightly and use as a topping for ice cream or other desserts.

You may keep this sauce in the refrigerator indefinitely.

Makes about 2 cups/500 ml.

Crema Pasticceria
Pastry Cream

This is a big-batch recipe, suitable for entertaining a large party. This cream is ideal for cream puffs, English trifle, fruit flan, or as a cake filling.

Homo or 2% milk	2 quarts	2 litres
Granulated sugar	2 cups	500 ml
Egg yolks	10	10
Butter	1 cup	250 ml
All-purpose flour	2 cups	500 ml
Vanilla extract	1/4 cup	60 ml
Grated peel of one orange		

In a heavy pot, combine milk with butter and half the sugar and bring to a boil. Combine remaining sugar with flour, add egg yolks and mix until smooth. Temper the egg mixture, add to the heated milk along with orange peel and return to a gentle boil. Cook over moderate low heat for 15 to 20 minutes, stirring frequently until thick.

Tip: If you find that the consistency is too thin, you may dilute 1 tbsp. of cornstarch in a bit of cold water and add to the cream while boiling.

Remove from heat and stir in vanilla. Cool, covered, in the refrigerator before using.

Makes about 12 cups/3 litres.

Crema Pasticceria Senza Latte
Milk-Free Pastry Cream

If you are lactose intolerant, this milk-free version of pastry cream works just as well as the original version above.

Water	3 cups	750 ml
Granulated sugar	3 cups	750 ml
Vegetable oil	1/4 cup	60 ml
Pineapple juice	2 cups	500 ml
Liquid honey	1/2 cup	120 ml
Vanilla extract	2 tbsp.	30 ml
Large eggs	3	3
All-purpose flour	1 cup	250 ml
Cornstarch	1/2 cup	120 ml

In a stainless steel saucepan, combine 2 cups (500 ml) of water, sugar, oil, pineapple juice, honey and vanilla. Bring to a boil. In a separate bowl, combine eggs with the flour, cornstarch and remaining water. Whisk together until smooth. Temper the egg mixture and add it to the saucepan, whisking constantly. Cook over moderate low heat for 15 to 20 minutes, stirring frequently until thick. Remove from heat and cool, covered, in the refrigerator. When cold, whisk again until smooth and glossy. Use right away or store in the refrigerator for up to 1 week.

Makes about 8 cups/2 litres.

Torta alla Pastorella
Ricotta Cheesecake

Eggs	6	6
Granulated sugar	2 cups	500 ml
All-purpose flour	1/3 cup	90 ml
Ricotta cheese	2 lbs.	900 g
Vegetable oil	1/2 cup	120 ml
Baking powder	2 tbsp.	30 ml
Vanilla extract	2 tbsp.	30 ml
Grated peel of 1 orange		

In a large bowl, beat eggs with sugar until light and foamy. Add flour and mix well. Add remaining ingredients and mix until well incorporated. Pour into a greased and floured 9-inch (22.5-cm) springform baking pan. Bake in a 375°F (190°C) oven for 55 minutes, or until firm. Cool in refrigerator before serving.

Makes 1 cake.

Banana alla Fiamma
Banana Flambé

You can flambé any choice of fruit using the same method.

Granulated sugar	1 cup	250 ml
Orange juice	1 cup	250 ml
Lemon juice	1/4 cup	60 ml
Unsalted butter	1/2 cup	120 ml
Bananas, peeled	6	6
Brandy or other liqueur	1/2 cup	120 ml

In a large fry pan, cook sugar over moderate heat until melted and lightly golden. Add juices and butter and continue cooking until the mixture takes on a honey-like consistency. Add the bananas and brandy and light with a match to set *en flambé*. Be careful to keep a fair distance from the pan as you light it, and tilt it away from your face, if possible. Once the alcohol has evaporated, simmer the bananas for a few minutes and serve warm.

Makes 3 large or 6 small servings.

Fragole Mona Lisa
Strawberries Mona Lisa

Fresh strawberries, hulled and sliced	2 pints	1 litre
Orange juice	1/2 cup	120 ml
Lemon juice	1/4 cup	60 ml
Liquid honey	1/2 cup	120 ml
Whipping cream	2 cups	500 ml
Chocolate sauce (see recipe, p. 168)	1/2 cup	120 ml
Walnuts or roasted almonds	1 cup	250 ml

In a large bowl, combine strawberries with juices and honey; mix well. Divide evenly between individual serving dishes, about 3/4 cup (180 ml) per person. In a separate bowl, whip cream until soft peaks appear. Spoon onto strawberries and top with chocolate syrup and nuts.

Makes 6 servings.

Zabaglione
Warm Custard with Sherry

Egg yolks	6	6
Granulated sugar	1/3 cup	90 ml
Sherry or Marsala wine	2/3 cup	150 ml
Water	1/4 cup	60 ml
Juice of 1/2 lemon		
Ladyfingers	12	12

In a stainless steel bowl, whisk together egg yolks, sugar, sherry, water and lemon juice. Whisk egg mixture over a simmering water bath until thick and foamy. Serve warm in champagne glasses accompanied with ladyfingers.

Makes 4 servings.

Crème Caramel
Sugared Custard

Caramel:

Sugar	1 cup	250 ml
Water	1/2 cup	120 ml

Custard:

Homo milk	1 quart	1 litre
Sugar	1 cup	250 ml
Vanilla extract	2 tbsp.	30 ml
Grated peel of 1 orange		
Eggs, beaten	8	8

To make the caramel, combine water and sugar in a saucepan and cook to a rich golden brown. Pour into individual, buttered ramekins and cool until caramel hardens. In a saucepan, bring milk, sugar, vanilla and the orange peel to a boil. Temper together the beaten eggs with the hot milk and remove from heat. Pour the custard into the ramekins. Place ramekins in a large baking pan and fill pan with enough water to come half way up the sides of the ramekins. Bake in a 325°F (165°C) oven for 45 minutes or until custard is firm and slightly golden on top. Refrigerate overnight before serving. To serve, run a knife around the rim of each ramekin to loosen the custard. Invert on a serving dish and shake gently until custard slides out.

Makes 10 servings.

Crêpes Suzette all'Ananas
Crêpes Suzettes with Pineapple

Granulated sugar	1 cup	250 ml
Sweet butter	1/2 cup	120 ml
Orange juice	3/4 cup	180 ml
Lemon juice	1/2 cup	120 ml
Fresh pineapple, peeled, cored, and diced	1	1
Brandy or Grand Marnier	1/2 cup	120 ml
Crêpes (see recipe, p. 146)	12	12

In a fry pan, melt the sugar over moderate heat until pale brown in colour. Add butter and juices and continue cooking until sauce is rich and honey-like. Add pineapple and brandy and light with a match to flambé. Be careful to keep your face away from the pan while lighting. Shake the pan until the flame dies down. Simmer for 3 to 5 minutes. Add the crêpes to the sauce and flip over, coating well. Fold into quarters and serve with sauce.

Makes 4 to 6 servings.

Tiramisu
Espresso Coffee Dessert

This is a large-batch recipe, suitable for entertaining a crowd.

Egg yolks	8	8
Granulated sugar	2 cups	500 ml
Amaretto liqueur or Marsala wine	1/2 cup	120 ml
All-purpose flour	2 tbsp.	30 ml
Espresso coffee	1 quart	1 litre
Mascarpone cheese	1 lb.	450 g
35% cream, whipped	1 quart	1 litre
Cocoa powder	1/2 cup	120 ml
Ladyfingers	6 dozen	6 dozen

In a stainless steel bowl, combine egg yolks, sugar, amaretto, flour, and half the coffee. Whisk over a simmering water bath until thick. Remove from heat and cool. When cold, add mascarpone and mix well, removing all lumps. Fold in the whipped cream. Brush the ladyfingers with the remainder of the coffee and line them in the bottom of a large baking dish. Pour in half the cheese mixture to cover the ladyfingers. Add another layer of ladyfingers and top with remaining half of cheese mixture. Sprinkle with cocoa powder and refrigerate two hours before serving.

Makes 12 servings.

Pan di Spagna
Sponge Cake

Eggs	14	14
Granulated sugar	2 cups	500 ml
Vegetable oil or melted butter	3/4 cup	180 ml
All-purpose flour	4 1/2 cups	1.2 litres
Milk or 10% cream	1 cup	250 ml
Vanilla extract	1/4 cup	60 ml
Baking powder	3 tbsp.	50 ml

In a stainless steel bowl, whisk together eggs and sugar until light and foamy. Add flour, milk and vanilla and continue mixing for 3 to 5 minutes. Add baking powder and mix an additional minute. Pour the batter into two greased and floured 8-inch (20-cm) baking dishes. Bake in a 350°F (175°C) oven for 50 to 55 minutes, or until fork inserted in middle comes out clean. Cool on a wire rack.

Makes two 8-inch (20-cm) cakes.

Index

175